KU-373-515

Crime Detection and
Prevention Series
Paper 92

New Heroin Outbreaks Amongst Young People in England and Wales

Howard Parker
Catherine Bury
Roy Egginton

Editor: Barry Webb
Home Office
Police Research Group
50 Queen Anne's Gate
London SW1H 9AT

© Crown Copyright 1998
First Published 1998

Police Research Group: Crime Detection and Prevention Series

The Home Office Police Research Group (PRG) was formed in 1992 to carry out and manage research in the social and management sciences relevant to the work of the police service. The terms of reference for the Group include the requirement to increase the influence of research and development work on police policy and practice.

The Crime Detection and Prevention Series follows on from the Crime Prevention Unit Papers, a series which has been published by the Home Office since 1983. The recognition that effective crime strategies will often involve both crime prevention and crime investigation, however, has led to the scope of this series being broadened. This new series will present research material on both crime prevention and crime detection in a way which informs policy and practice throughout the service.

A parallel series of papers on crime prevention is also published by PRG, as is a periodical on policing research called 'Focus'.

ISBN 1-84082-129-9

Copies of this publication can be available in formats accessible to the visually impaired on request.

Foreword

It is important that the police and other agencies involved in crime prevention have the capacity to respond to emerging new problems quickly and effectively. The nature and size of crime problems change over time, and we need to have in place systems that enable potential new problems to be identified and 'nipped in the bud'.

This paper provides an example of an early warning system in relation to drug misuse. The 'rapid audit' reported here shows evidence of a spread of heroin use amongst young people which signals the need for action now to prevent this developing into a major problem. The report also suggests how a more systematic early warning system might be developed.

This is an important report. Its findings and implications will be considered carefully by the UK Anti-Drugs Coordinator in taking forward the anti-drugs strategy, and the police, health services and Drug Action Teams also need to take note of it in developing local drug strategies.

S W BOYS SMITH
Director of Police Policy
Home Office
July 1998

Acknowledgements

The successful completion of this report has been totally dependent on the goodwill and cooperation of literally hundreds of people. We would like to thank all the police officers, DAT officials and local professionals who made survey returns, gave telephone interviews and welcomed us to their areas for fieldwork visits. Thanks also to the young heroin users who agreed to be interviewed.

Special thanks to Neil Matthews of Manchester Regional Research Laboratories for the mapping, to Dianne Moss for processing and to Ed Jurith. At the Home Office, Charlie Lloyd, Malcolm Ramsay, Warwick Maynard, Jessica Jacobson, Barry Webb and John Corkery have all helped our endeavours. Thanks also to Jim Fitzpatrick at the UK ADCU and Alistair Thomas at the Department of Health.

Howard Parker
Catherine Bury
Roy Egginton

The Authors

Howard Parker is Professor of Social Work and director of SPARC in the Department of Social Policy and Social Work at Manchester University. Catherine Bury and Roy Egginton are researchers at SPARC.

PRG would like to thank Professor Mike Hough of South Bank University for acting as independent assessor for this report.

Executive summary

- Many areas in Britain were the sites of major heroin outbreaks during the mid 1980s. Merseyside, Greater Manchester, London, the Scottish cities and towns down the western side of Britain were most affected. These outbreaks involved a **minority** of 18-25 year olds who were predominantly unemployed and lived in deprived urban areas. Their heroin careers lasted many years and users routinely became deeply involved in acquisitive crime, drug dealing and prostitution to supplement state benefits in funding expensive habits. This in turn caused community damage and placed enormous pressure on local policing and criminal justice services, social care and health budgets. Most areas eventually set up methadone-led treatment services to 'manage' this population of long term users.

- Whilst such 'heavy end' drugs careers continue, the 1990s has been dominated by the extensive 'recreational' use of drugs like cannabis, amphetamines and ecstasy, particularly by youth populations. During the first half of the 1990s heroin was eschewed by most young people as a highly addictive drug used only by 'junkies'. However, since around 1996 signs, indicators and rumours that heroin is making a return have been building.

- As a consequence and in the continuing absence of any other 'early warning systems' this audit was commissioned. It involved a national postal survey of all police forces and Drug Action Teams (DATs) in England and Wales. Over two hundred separate returns were received from police, probation, social services, doctors, drugs services, outreach workers, etc. thanks to excellent networking by local DATs. Eventually returns were made by 73% of DATs and 86% of police forces. The survey was supplemented by extensive telephone interviewing and fieldwork visits to numerous towns and cities to interview local professionals and young heroin users.

- This research focused on 'under 19s' (so does not provide the whole heroin picture) and was concerned with the perceived **spread** of new heroin outbreaks. It cannot quantify or enumerate the number of users, which remains unknown even to the affected areas. 80% of DAT networks and 81% of police forces making returns reported recent or new clusters or, in some cases, full scale outbreaks of heroin use within their jurisdictions. This is an unprecedented spread profile which the report maps in detail.

- These outbreaks are not currently occurring in the old heroin areas (e.g. N.W. England, London) nor in many rural areas but they are colonising in most regions of England, particularly N.E. England, Yorkshire, West Midlands, Avon and S.W. England. The first outbreaks began around 1993-4 primarily in large towns/small cities with a heroin 'footprint' from the past (e.g. established user/dealer networks). However heroin use is now occurring in completely new areas with no heroin history and the spread pattern suggests many communities will see its arrival during this and next year. Young people in these areas initially have only limited understanding of heroin's potency and dependency potential.

- The most pernicious feature of this outbreak is the evidence that it is supply led. The UK has seen a major illegal importation of heroin from S.W. Asia brought primarily via the Balkan route on across the EU into this country. A fall in price, strong availability, with purity remaining high, all indicate a sustained supply. Heroin has been actively marketed as 'brown', as smokable and in £5 and £10 deals in new markets. Distributors use the motorway networks to link the 'kilo' middle level suppliers often found in the old heroin cities, with the 'ounces' dealers and on to the town level, home based and 'mobile' dealers. A £10 bag contains one tenth to one sixteenth of a gram of heroin with a 20%-50% purity. With an ounce of heroin costing around £800 and producing over 300 £10 wraps destined for the street user-buyer, profits are enormous at all points in the supply and distribution chain. This ensures the heroin market makers are highly determined, increasingly sophisticated and thus particularly difficult to apprehend and convict. Moreover 'taking out' heroin dealers at the local level rarely stems local supply as replacement dealerships quickly emerge. This suggests a far more sophisticated approach is required whereby a multi-agency strategy is called for at the local level and a co-ordinated national and 'cross border' policing approach is needed to disrupt the heroin distribution systems which network the country.

- Most of the new young users taking up heroin use can be described as 'socially excluded', coming from the poorest parts of the affected towns and cities. However, there is a spectrum of susceptibility and clear signs of a broader penetration with heroin use being found amongst 'bonded' in education/in work youth from more affluent families. This section of new users tend to come from those involved in the serious end of recreational drug use. There is some evidence of heroin being used as a 'chill out' drug by young adult clubbers. Currently more young men than young women are trying heroin. Ethnic minority populations have been affected. Most new users begin by smoking and 'chasing' heroin but a significant move towards injecting is widely reported in the survey.

- The age of onset (first trying) has been falling for all drug initiation but it must be of particular concern that a significant proportion (over a third) of the 'under

19s' age group were described as under 16 years of age. This suggests that the overall at risk age group should be defined as 14-25 years.

- Although the government's new drugs strategy will eventually involve a major investment in drugs services, there is currently a dearth of services for young people in general and heroin users in particular. This means there will be an unfortunate time lag between planning and opening new services which will seriously hamper local responses. Despite this, very careful safeguards are needed in setting up new services. Automatically modelling new services on methadone prescribing may be ill-advised; it may be more appropriate to provide a young person centred, 'user friendly' intake and assessment, street level service which assesses the local problem before channelling young problem users to more tailored specialist services including needle exchanges, harm reduction strategies, detoxification, social and employment skills training and, where necessary, the prescribing of methadone. These new services must be comprehensively 'quality assured' and far more focused than many current services.

- This research maps what may be the early stages of a second wave of heroin outbreaks. Further research and monitoring is required to quantify the degree of penetration, spread potential and likely outcomes in terms of problems for young users, drug related crime and demand on local services. Action research at the local level will also help promote good practice. DATs are crying out for 'good practice' guidelines in responding to the spread of heroin.

Contents

List of figures

List of maps

List of tables

1. The high costs of heroin outbreaks

From anecdote to evidence

Stories about new cohorts of young heroin users emerging, primarily on deprived housing estates, began to be told from around 1994-5. The storytellers lived or worked on the 'front line'. Thus community activists, youth and community and outreach workers, local journalists and of course police officers were the first to suggest 'smack' was finding its way into new local youth populations.

Initially these concerns about heroin outbreaks for instance in the Welsh valleys, Bristol and a few towns in NE England, seemed to be describing atypical, isolated scenes. Only a few years earlier we had been told that crack cocaine would grip Britain's towns and cities (Kleber, 1988; Stutman, 1989). Yet the crack epidemic never unfolded, although crack use has expanded since (Parker and Bottomley, 1996).

However, these heroin stories, although much less publicised, did not go away but instead, during 1996-7, became more widespread. For instance, police, drugs worker and inter-agency conferences often became the venues for informal information sharing. Delegates began to find their heroin stories were matched by colleagues from elsewhere (eg ACPO Drugs Conference, 1997). Given all this and the emergence of some indirect evidence from official indicators (eg. new to treatment profiles, drugs seizures) suggesting a **trend** of increases in heroin use, the case for researching the situation strengthened through 1997 leading to the audit described in this report.

An audit of the new heroin outbreaks

Unlike the Netherlands or the USA, the United Kingdom has no integrated 'early warning systems' to identify and monitor significant changes in illicit drug use. Whilst ISDD (e.g. 1997) has a clear mandate to collate secondary data from all the key sources and plot trends for public scrutiny there is no clear expectation these will help inform forward planning and the allocation of prevention, treatment and enforcement resources.

This report describes how in the absence of any other device an audit was quickly undertaken to assess the scale and nature of these apparent, late 1990s, heroin outbreaks amongst 'under 19s' in England and Wales. Using basic social science research methods the audit's primary aim was to assess the validity of the claim that heroin use was extending beyond the longer term endemic populations created during the 1980s and penetrating new youth populations.

Specific objectives involved:

- Mapping where these outbreaks involved sizeable populations of young people for England and Wales.
- Describing the characteristics of the new, late 1990s, young heroin users.
- Outlining how heroin is being marketed and supplied to youth populations and describing its street level price and purity.
- Describing and assessing the initial official responses in those areas (eg. towns) affected by these outbreaks.
- Attempting to forecast the spread potential of these outbreaks given heroin's previous association with 'epidemic' diffusion patterns.
- Defining any further research and monitoring programmes needed to inform policy and practice responses.
- Commenting on the development of services for young heroin users.

Youth and drugs experience during the 1990s

Little new has been said or written about heroin during the 1990s certainly in terms of youth populations. Whilst we continue to describe and explore the, now endemic, longer term heroin using populations which developed during the 1980s, this is primarily in respect of treatment options (NTORS, 1996), changes in route of heroin administration (eg. Griffiths et al, 1994), the heroin-methadone-crime relationships (Hough, 1996; Parker and Kirby, 1996) and the spread of HIV/AIDS (eg. Gossop et al, 1993).

Heroin did not go away during the 1990s. We have continued to see a trickle of 'incidence', new cases, involving *young* heroin users through the decade. These clusters have been found mainly in the traditional heroin sites which developed during the 1980s. These sites continue to host consecutive age cohorts of young heroin users. However the numbers have been relatively small and the characteristics of the users widely recognised. Basically the profile of new young heroin users emerging during the first half of the 1990s can be defined as 'from the margins'. They are primarily care leavers, persistent offenders and educational under-achievers who have had impoverished and/or damaged childhoods (Carlen, 1996; Parker and Buchanan, 1996; Graham and Bowling, 1996). Essentially they live in subcultural worlds (Collison, 1996). In post-modern terminology they epitomise social exclusion and life at the margins (Coffield et al, 1986).

Their fate has not been a **Big Issue** both because their numbers have been so small and their heroin and poly-drug use has not spread into the wider normative, youth population.

Indeed one of the defining characteristics of the literally millions of 1990s young people who have tried or use illicit drugs has been their rejection of heroin, of crack cocaine and of injecting. Up to half of all young people in England and Wales, who have grown up during the mid 1990s will have tried an illicit drug by young adulthood (Plant and Miller, 1996; Roberts et al, 1995; Parker et al, 1998). Yet since probably less than 2% will have tried heroin it is unsurprising that today's, late 1990s, youth know little about opiates. They do not remember the 1980s with the 'junkie' as folk devil and his syringe and needle as a transmitter of HIV, AIDS and death. Only a small minority of today's young Britons have grown up in established heroin communities. The vast majority have had few contacts with the contemporary heroin addicts or lived next door to a chaotic 'smack family' by way of drugs education. Moreover heroin has been largely excluded from the main anti-drug public health campaigns in England (HEA) and Wales (Health Promotion Wales). And finally it can be argued that parents, teachers and state officials, by too often arguing that all illicit drugs are bad and dangerous, have failed to distinguish *between* drugs. If we imply that cannabis and heroin are both equally dangerous yet focus on cannabis we should not be surprised if young people underestimate the potency of heroin use since most hold benign attitudes towards cannabis (Parker et al, 1998).

In short despite the unprecedented increase in drugs experience of contemporary youth their drugs wisdom fails them in relation to heroin and does so increasingly with each 1990s adolescent year group. Official interventions have inadvertently exacerbated this situation by failing to distinguish sufficiently between illicit drugs and their relative dangers. In the end this means a proportion of today's youth, by not having 'nuf respect' for heroin, are susceptible to what, as we shall see in Section 5 is a supply led enticement to try heroin.

Post war heroin outbreaks in the UK

Epidemic spread
Recent history tells us that the age group most susceptible to beginning heroin use has been about 16 - 25 years. However only a small minority of such an age cohort will ever try heroin and only a proportion of these will become regular heroin users. Thus even where a full blown heroin outbreak occurs in a particular city, town or urban area we would only expect to find about 5 per thousand of the adult population involved or less than 10% of the 'at risk' age

group. We have thus far no documented experience in the UK of a heroin outbreak extending beyond these proportions.

Whilst we have seen heroin use develop in a particular town or city slowly and incrementally another lesson from post war drugs 'history' is that heroin use has a strong tendency to grow in an **epidemic** fashion. Although there are some dangers in using this term it does succinctly capture the way heroin use spreads rapidly both socially and geographically.

This type of drug spread was first fully documented in the USA when a series of full blown, post war, heroin epidemics affected many American cities. The basic model developed by Hunt and Chambers (1976) and Hughes et al (1977) was tested and revised for the UK by Parker et al (1988) and Fazey (1987).

Basically heroin epidemics start unnoticed but spread very rapidly. Two processes are at work. **Microdiffusion** involves the spread through personal contact. More experienced users facilitate novices, the 'knowledge' about price, purity, how to smoke, chase or inject, what feelings to look for, etc., are passed on between associates and friendship networks. In a full blown epidemic this diffusion occurs simultaneously on numerous sites. Thus density is increased as the results of micro diffusion join up initially, primarily, in densely populated urban areas. Over time several heroin sites develop in one town or city but not only do they 'join up' they also through **macro diffusion**, spread to neighbouring areas. Clearly supplier and dealer movement to avoid surveillance or open a new market, is one method of macro diffusion. The migration of users to another 'quieter' area or town is another.

The remarkable thing about this initially American model was its applicability to the UKs 1980s heroin outbreaks discussed in the next section. Parker et al (1988) undertook a four year study of the heroin epidemic on the Wirral, Merseyside. Figure 1 illustrates how Wirral with a population of 340,000 moved from having almost no heroin users at the beginning of the 1980s to about 4,000 young adult users six years later. The new cases (incidence) peak over a few years but because few heroin users give up in the short run the number of users in the community at any particular time (prevalence) continues to rise for several years. The consequences for communities hosting a full blown heroin outbreak thus last many years and at enormous social and economic cost as the UK discovered during the last 'cycle' over a decade ago.

Figure 1 Model of the Wirral Heroin 'Epidemic'

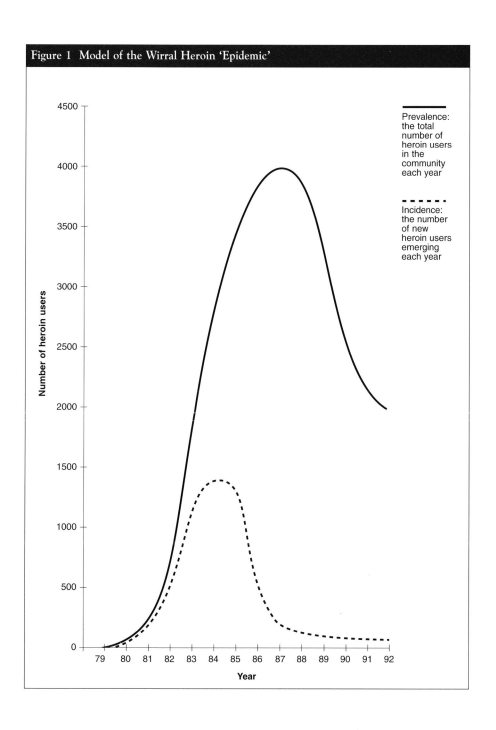

The 'costs' of the 1980s heroin outbreaks

Links to poverty and deprivation
During the 1960s and 1970s most UK heroin users were London based. They were twenty and thirty something and their drug use was part of a hippie lifestyle or bohemian subculture (Stimson and Oppenheimer, 1982). Whilst occasional heroin 'outbreaks' affecting certain towns and cities did occur (de Alceron, 1969), these were rare.

The full blown heroin 'epidemics' which affected American cities in the post war period were unknown to the UK until the 1980s. Then for the first time several cities and urban conurbations in England and Scotland found themselves hosting major heroin outbreaks. These new heroin users were young (18-25 years) initially primarily male and came from deprived urban environments. The new heroin users (Pearson et al, 1986; Parker et al, 1988) were basically poor, undereducated, unemployed, 'marginalised' young men. These heroin epidemics centred on Merseyside (Parker et al, 1988; Fazey, 1987), Greater Manchester, Glasgow (Haw, 1985), Edinburgh, parts of London (Hartnoll et al, 1985) and to a lesser extent Bristol (Gay et al, 1985). By the mid 1980s these outbreaks had spread to other towns and cities but primarily on the west side of the Pennines and down into Wales rather than the east side of the British Isles. Map 1 (see Section 3) based on treatment numbers in the late 1980s gives some indication of the epidemiological spread. Clearly notifications of those 'addicted' to heroin and receiving treatment is not an ideal indicator but by 1989 and with the HIV/AIDS 'scare', quite a high proportion of heroin users were in treatment and this map does give a reasonable picture of the main heroin sites. This history of the geography of the last heroin epidemic is, as we shall see, central to understanding the epidemiology of the current, late 1990s, outbreaks.

Drug related crime
Whilst the relationships between illicit drug use and crime are many and complex (Edmunds et al. 1998; Parker, 1996; Hough, 1996; Hammersley et al, 1989) there is little doubt that heroin supplying and use is closely connected to crime. The international market for supplying heroin and the role of dealers and user -dealers within the UK is characterised by a drugs for profit ethos (Stares, 1996). As importantly, given heroin outbreaks since the early 1980s have disproportionately affected poor people in deprived communities (ACMD, 1998), dependent users thus have a strong tendency to resort to acquisitive crime, notably burglary, shoplifting, fraud and theft (Jarvis and Parker, 1989; Bennett, 1998). Whilst the role of social security benefits, wages, cash-in-hand work, and reliance on partners

or the sex industry must not be underestimated (ISDD, 1994) the role of acquisitive crime is immense. Even if only a half of an urban heroin or combination drug user's bill is funded by acquisitive crime, the levels of offending required to meet the other half of an annual drugs bill is daunting. With drugs bills in excess of £10,000 a year (Brain et al, 1997) then once we start counting dependent users in their hundreds or thousands the impact of the dependent user - drug driven crime relationship is awesome even if many of these people were involved in offending prior to dependent drug use.

Dependent drugs careers, personal and social damage
Throughout the 1980s in terms of dependent heroin use, and, into the 1990s in respect of 'heavy end' combination drug use, including crack cocaine, there is ample evidence that problem drug careers produce much collateral damage. This damage is primarily associated with the deviant *lifestyles* which dependent, heavy end, drug users move into (Walters, 1994). When poor, young adults, from the margins, get involved in drug careers they cannot easily walk away from, then whatever the positives of heroin use, a series of dire consequences tend to follow them.

A much reported phenomenon concerns the damage to or often breakdown of relationships within families. Indeed the mid 1980s saw a spectacular rise in the number of self help groups for mothers of young heroin users (Dorn et al, 1987) which bore witness to the traumas of having children steal from and lie to their parents about money and drugs, of unpaid dealers putting in windows, of dramatic arrests, of sons and daughters remanded in custody (Parker et al, 1988). Having left or been excluded from the relative security and structure of familial homes, young users would then classically find themselves either in sink housing or stumble into problematic romantic relationships.

Young women would often become involved in shoplifting or prostitution. They would often have drug using boyfriends who sometimes pulled them further into criminal careers as home based dealers. Being pregnant whilst addicted to heroin would routinely trigger child protection enquiries. Young heroin mothers then suffered stigmatising responses and, in fairness, some really could not, there and then, make good enough parents (Klenka, 1986; Kearnery and Ibbetson, 1991).

Young men got further involved in drug dealing, theft and burglary to fund growing drugs bills, whether for the first time or through amplified criminal careers. Once on this slide dependent users found structure and conformity harder and harder to sustain. Court cases continue to mount up and further periods of custody follow.

Such significant life events began to motivate increasing numbers to seek treatment (Power et al, 1992). However with enormous public concern about HIV/AIDS and needle sharing, the development of a plethora of 'user friendly' service initiatives, centred on methadone and needle exchange, were put in place by the mid to late 1980s. The hidden sector of users gradually shrank as far more longer term heroin users went into treatment.

Whilst such treatment initiatives have undoubtedly helped manage this population and certainly reduced their offending rates (Hough, 1996), many of these drug careers, supported by prescribed methadone, have persisted right through the users' 'twenties' before any signs of maturing or burning out of their deviant lifestyles. Many eventually speak with a fatalism and despair about their drug journeys and how, in the end, the bad times far outweigh the good (Brain et al, 1997).

Summary

As anecdotal evidence mounted during 1997 that heroin use was again on the increase and particularly amongst youth populations, this study was commissioned. Its basic purpose was to ascertain the extent to which towns and cities in England and Wales were hosting new heroin outbreaks. It was also designed to describe the characteristics of any new clusters of young heroin users and the way any new heroin supply and distribution markets were developing. It was also hoped the study would define whether these outbreaks were isolated clusters or more worryingly, symptomatic of a more serious heroin 'epidemic'.

The 1980s heroin epidemics deeply affected urban NW England, parts of London and the Scottish cities, with further spread into north Wales and many towns on the west side of England. The consequences of dependent heroin use which primarily captured a proportion of young adult, unemployed people from the country's most deprived areas, was dire during the 1980s. Most heroin users became entangled in deviant lifestyles which involved prostitution, drug dealing and a large amount of acquisitive crime. Breakdowns in family relationships were common and in the most affected areas heroin dependency became a child protection issue. Many users themselves had difficult and unhappy lives during their 'twenties'. Treatment services dominated by methadone had to be developed at considerable cost to the public purse to manage this problematic population, most of whom, by the end of the eighties, had entered treatment at least once.

For all these reasons heroin outbreaks cannot be ignored. Heroin is not, as many apparently **drugwise** young people in this study initially presumed, just another drug.

2. Early warnings of emerging drug scenes

Because of its illicit and illegal nature the use of controlled substances is largely hidden from scrutiny. Drug users and drug dealers tend to keep their activities a secret. Moreover, whilst one can go into a pub or club and count the number of smokers or drinkers, it is not normally feasible, aside from cannabis, to observe the use of ecstasy, amphetamines or cocaine, for example. The administration of these drugs will have been discreet or secretive. Indeed, unless illicit drug users are arrested, fall ill or seek help they are unlikely to appear on any data-bases or ever be asked to disclose their drug use.

With substantial increases in illegal drug experimentation and use in recent years and an increase in both the range and overall availability of illicit drugs, it is important that the UK has some means of monitoring its drugs scenes and trends. Some drugs are particularly dangerous. Over the last decade well over a thousand young people in Great Britain have died from trying volatile substances like solvents and gases. The development of the highly addictive crack cocaine and its epidemic spread in many cities in the USA could, for instance, repeat itself in parts of Europe, leading to major crime, health and social problems.

Policy makers need drug misuse early warning systems to prepare and allocate primary and secondary prevention measures in education, health, drugs services and crime reduction. With new designer drugs appearing almost every year it is important to quickly identify the emergence of new drugs of use, particularly if the drugs have toxic or other harmful side effects. With an increasing tendency towards combination drug use or poly-drug use it is vital to keep a close eye on the effects of such drug repertories which may be life threatening or may lead to dangerous or violent behaviour towards others.

Perhaps the severest lesson about early warning requirements was given by the heroin epidemic of the 1980's discussed in the last section. It took several years to define and map and even longer to respond to. In retrospect, the cost to the communities involved and to the public purse could have been reduced had official responses homed in earlier.

USA 'Early Warning Systems'

The USA has the most sophisticated network of drug monitoring and early warning systems – DAWN, DUF and *Pulse Check*.

The Department of Health and Human Services' (HHS) Drug Abuse Warning Network (DAWN) was begun in the early 1970's and includes two samples. One is a random representative sample of hospital emergency departments; the other of coroner's offices. The purpose of DAWN is to monitor trends in drug related episodes and deaths. It also measures the health consequences of drug use and changes in the character and extent of the use of drugs.

In 1996, a total of 612 hospitals were selected for the DAWN sample and 452 hospital emergency departments (74 percent) participated in the survey. Within each facility participating in DAWN, a designated reporter, usually a member of the emergency department or medical records staff, is responsible for identifying drug-related episodes and recording and submitting the data for each case. To be eligible for inclusion in DAWN, the emergency or death, must be induced by or related to drug use, regardless of whether the ingestion occurred minutes or hours before the episode. A 'case' involves the non medical use of a legal drug or any use of an illegal drug; and the reasons for taking the substance can be for either dependence, a suicide attempt, or psychic effects. The latest DAWN issued in December, 1997, showed a decrease in overall drug-related hospital emergency department episodes from 1995 to 1996.

The US Department of Justice conducts the Drug Use Forecasting (DUF) program to calculate the percentage of individuals arrested for crimes whose urine sample indicate drug use. DUF provides snapshots of the extent of drug use among the criminal justice system population and relationships between drug use and crime. The DUF panel includes 23 major metropolitan areas. In 1996 DUF program collected data from 19,835 male arrests and 7,532 female arrestees. Data from 4,145 juvenile males and 645 juvenile females were also collected in 1996. Recent DUF data, for example, has highlighted the dramatic drop in drug -related homicides in US cities. The DUF system is being renovated and will become ADAM (Arrestee Drug Abuse Monitoring).

The White House Office of National Drug Control Policy (ONDCP) issues the twice yearly Pulse Check report of national trends in illicit drug use and drug markets. The Pulse Check report draws on discussions with approximately 75 ethnographers and epidemiologists working in the drug field, law enforcement personnel, and drug treatment providers to provide timely information about changes and trends in drug scenes as they develop. The Pulse Check examines approximately 12 major drug using US cities in each report. Recent Pulse Check reports have indicated a rise in heroin misuse among younger users in the US.

Drugs indicators in the United Kingdom

Although compared to the USA the UK appears to have no purpose-built early warning and drug trend monitoring system, it does have numerous indicators which are potentially helpful. Indeed aside from the Netherlands, the UK's drugs indicators are relatively sophisticated in European terms. The difficulty is that they operate for other purposes, each uses distinctive and idiosyncratic measuring rods and there is a significant time lag before the figures are processed and published.

In this section we assess how these indicators currently operate and if they could be improved to identify and monitor new drug trends. In short, could the 'prompts' and stimuli for this investigation have been created by a critical analytic overview of current drug indicators and could they have been interrogated to collect the sort of information and picture we present in this study?

The United Kingdom has a range of data bases which report information about drug use and related activity including data regarding treatment, drug seizures, arrest data, hospital data, and drug related mortalities. In this analysis we will limit ourselves to the most likely potential early warning indictors.

Traditionally two separate Home Office Statistical Bulletins have been produced annually to publish statistical trends on drugs controlled by the Misuse of Drugs Act 1971. One relied on the 'Addicts Index' which collated reports by medical practitioners on patients seen and described by drug of addiction, treatment regime, age and sex of addict, injecting status and source of the notification. The Addicts Index was closed in April 1997 however. The other Bulletin reports on seizures of controlled drugs and persons dealt with for offences involving controlled drugs.

The closure of the Addicts Index was logical in that it overlapped with the other help-seeking, treatment-led indicator, The Regional Drug Misuse Databases, overseen by the Department of Health. This system utilises a regional reporting structure based on returns from specialist drug and alcohol agencies, GPs, police surgeons, some hospital departments and prison medical officers. Annual reports are available through the Department of Health's Statistical Bulletin. Regional returns provide data referring to the sex of individuals, area of the return, drugs misused, injecting behaviour and agency treatment episodes.

Utilising current indicators

Can or could these help-seeking and enforcement indicators be effective in predicting and mapping significant and new drug scenes? Turning first to the Regional Drug Misuse Database we can see that there was an increase in young drug users starting agency episodes over the three years from 31 March 1993. During this period the number of users aged under 19 starting agency episodes increased by 778 episodes, a 35% increase (see Figure 2).

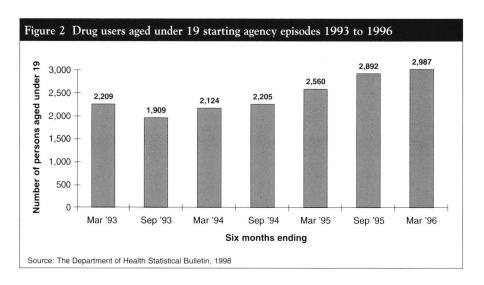

Figure 2 Drug users aged under 19 starting agency episodes 1993 to 1996

Source: The Department of Health Statistical Bulletin, 1998

Over this three year period, the percentage of users who used heroin as their main drug increased from 47% to 54% at the end of the period (see Figure 3).

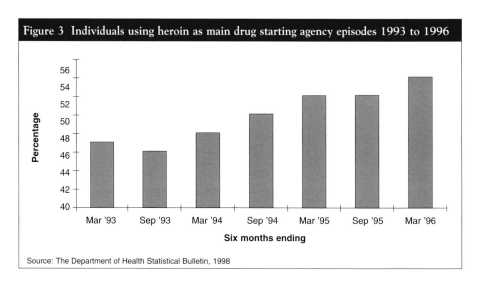

Figure 3 Individuals using heroin as main drug starting agency episodes 1993 to 1996

Source: The Department of Health Statistical Bulletin, 1998

Advantages of the Regional Data Base System

One of the main advantages of the data base statistics is that they are regionally sensitive and can provide a more comprehensive picture than any other comparable statistical data set of the habits of help seeking drug users. For instance, the number of individual users per 100,000 population by regional office area under the age of twenty starting new agency episodes in the period 1 October 1995 to 31 March 1996 was 56 in the Northern and Yorkshire District; this figure was more than twice the average figure (24) for all other regions and more than twice the number for the next highest scoring region, which was North West (24) . This rise in the Yorkshire figures would suggest changes are occurring in this region.

Limitations of the Regional Data Base System

Unfortunately, the regional data base system has a number of limitations as other commentators have recognised (Hickman et al 1997). First, there is a time lag between data collection and publication. Secondly, it often takes many years for people to first approach a treatment service, and where they do seek help there is usually a significant time lag since the beginning of their problematic drug use. Thirdly, many people will never seek treatment, and will not be represented in these figures.

Another problem with comparing the data base figures is that the regional data bases do not all use the same computer software, and analysis at national level is therefore not straightforward.

The overriding problem however, is that there is no mandatory obligation for professionals to 'notify' a treatment episode. Consequently this system substantially under reports drug users in treatment. Worst of all it does this in ways which distort the overall picture. Non compliance is greater in some areas than others because of regional relationships. Some areas have more treatment services than others and some areas have very large treatment centres which do or do not report efficiently. This all affects the veracity of area returns. This is not to say that this system could not be revamped and improved, However, this would require new investment and new regulation. In the end however even with upgrading this recording system it is much better at measuring long term trends rather than identifying new developments. As we have shown, the signs of an increase in young users appear gradual and incremental in the data base statistics. As we shall see this is not the case – far more epidemiological change has occurred.

Seizure data

The **number** of annual seizures involving heroin have been rising continuously since the early 1990's (see Figure 4). Between 1995 and 1996, seizures involving heroin rose by 3,300 to 9,800 (up by 52 per cent).

The **quantity** of heroin seized in 1996 was 1,070kg which represented a decrease of 23 per cent from the previous year (see Figure 4) but was still the second largest quantity ever to be recorded. Approximately seven tenths was recovered from H.M. Customs which is similar to previous years.

The number of police seizures of heroin increased from 6,330 to 9,680 (53 per cent) over the same period. All but four of the 52 police forces recorded greater numbers of heroin seizures. The largest increase was in West Yorkshire where it doubled to 1,360.

Although heroin purity was sometimes greater during the 1980s, figures for purity levels for heroin seized during the 1990s have climbed across the decade. Most recently the average purity of heroin seized by the police in 1996 and analysed by the Forensic Science Service laboratories was at about 44 per cent.

The seizure data described above do suggest an increase in supply (and perhaps demand) for heroin and would suggest a sharp upturn in heroin use as a consequence.

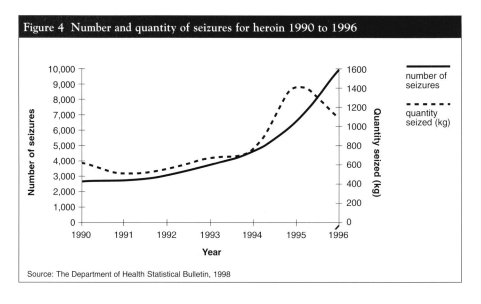

Figure 4 Number and quantity of seizures for heroin 1990 to 1996

Source: The Department of Health Statistical Bulletin, 1998

'Offender' data

The number of 'drug offenders' (which includes those people cautioned, found guilty or dealt with by compounding) rose steadily from the eighties until 1992, thereafter the figures have risen more steeply. The number of offenders in 1996 who had committed offences involving heroin in particular was 5,900, which was 40 per cent up on the 1995 figure and a four fold increase on the 1992 figure.

Offenders aged under 21 represented about 34 per cent all of offenders in 1996, approximately the same as the 1995 figure. The figures for drug offenders aged under 21 have increased since the beginning of the 1990's with a slight decline in 1996. In 1990 the figure stood at 16,185 and has increased almost two fold in 1996. (see Figure 5). 'Offender' data do therefore suggest an increase of heroin possession and supplying is occurring on the ground.

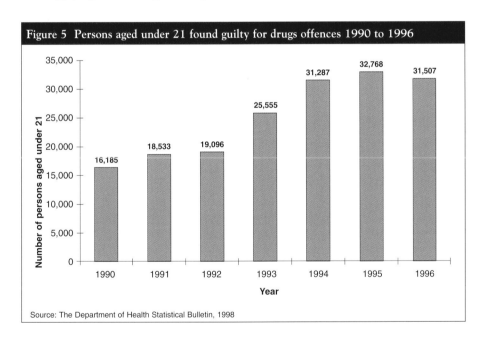

Figure 5 Persons aged under 21 found guilty for drugs offences 1990 to 1996

Source: The Department of Health Statistical Bulletin, 1998

Limitations of enforcement statistics

The debate about the veracity of police statistics is a complex one (Bottomley and Pease 1986), and need not be rehearsed here save to say they can only be a secondary 'rough' indicator of a new drugs scene. At the local level they can be usefully utilised and interpreted by multi-disciplinary networks trying to define their local drugs status. As a key national warning sensor they are limited by each force's own policing priorities, enforcement procedures and recording systems. They do not contextualise the trends with clear up rates or reports of 'lucky strikes' or indeed intensive pro-active operations.

The absence of effective drugs indicators
Our overall conclusion is that the UK has no current way of identifying and monitoring a new drugs scene. Existing data base and recording systems have all been set up for other purposes and our expectations of them have grown because we lack dedicated early warning beacons. Even if we adjust and upgrade the existing drug data collecting tools to spot new scenes, these data sets are best seen as secondary indictors to be cross referenced with a more purpose-built system.

A jigsaw early warning system

Figure 6 illustrates who should be involved in the operation of a tailor-made early warning system.

The basic principle is that for an early warning system to function successfully it must have sensors close to sites of new use. Thus front line indicators close to the community and street level and able to detect local developments are essential. In this model local Accident and Emergency Departments would ideally have a role in reporting deaths, overdoses, and drug related accidents. Similarly as GP's are increasingly encouraged to treat drug misusers they must be expected to contribute to better data collection. There is little doubt that GPs are currently seeing many new young heroin users, yet the scale of this remains unknown.

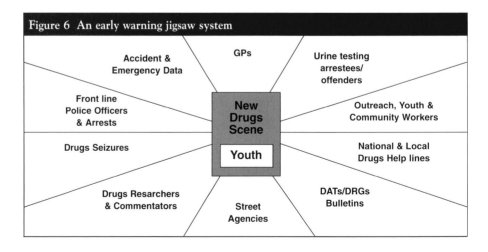

Figure 6 An early warning jigsaw system

The reality which would have to be faced, however, is that both these potential medical indicators\informants are notoriously non-compliant in respect of recording and reporting drug treatment episodes and it is doubtful whether this could be cost-effectively changed.

However, other front line professionals such as police officers, outreach workers and street agency staff could and probably would provide up-to-date intelligence if it was collected appropriately and the effort rewarded, perhaps by a small fee and, most of all, feedback which they in turn would find useful. Such front-line indicators could be linked to the local DAT /DRGs since here again we have a network of professionals who should be able to identify new drug trends fairly quickly. It would only be when we put all 100+ 'bulletins' together, say twice yearly, that the added value of a national picture would be harvested. This could presumably be a role for the UK Anti-Drugs Coordination Unit.

Pulse Check in the USA successfully pulls together ethnographers and front line workers/drugs researchers to share observations on changing drugs scenes. Moreover, since the Dutch have also produced such a system in Amsterdam it should be possible to create such a network in the UK. This would allow for early results from large scale household surveys, notably the national crime surveys (e.g. Ramsay and Spiller, 1997), self report survey findings (e.g. Balding, 1998) and qualitative studies, to be collated to identify any changes in drugs consumption. For instance, a series of longitudinal school based surveys and confidential interviews undertaken between 1995 and 1998 appear to indicate an upturn in heroin trying amongst 14-16 year olds (Aldridge et al, forthcoming)

There is tremendous potential for Helplines to play a key role in providing early indications of new drug trends and related problems. Although the National Drugs Helpline currently only 'data bases' 10% of its calls it could, with a new contract specification, monitor all calls and provide information about the age, gender and geographical location of callers: by drug and by self-assessed problem or issue. The NDH has identified an upturn in 'heroin' calls in the past year which suggests it would be a key piece of the jigsaw. Similarly, Parent Helplines at a local level, usually run by the voluntary sector, could be contracted to provide comparable data.

Finally, with the new initiatives in the urine testing of arrestees and supervised offenders being likely to extend, we have a further potentially robust indicator which could become a key piece in the jigsaw particularly in respect of monitoring any relationships between drug use and offending (Bennett, 1998).

With such a system in place we could then see how seizure data, particularly if contextualised and supplemented by Customs and Excise and International Intelligence, could be utilised effectively. Treatment data and 'offender' data would probably be of greatest value at the regional or local level where these systems would operate. They would also act as a validator of longer term trends.

Feasibility
Aside from the difficulties of co-opting busy primary and emergency medical practitioners into a local system there is little doubt that a jigsaw network would produce an effective early warning system using local pictures to create a national montage. The doubt must be whether such a system could be set up, currently, given the differing agendas and priorities and traditional demarcations between government departments at the centre and the complexities of funding the front line partners at the local level. Whilst there is clearly a move towards co-ordination vis-a-vis drugs policy and drugs related expenditure we are probably several years away from having the corporate ethos and command and communication status required to run such a system effectively as a mainstream activity.

Summary

Despite the apparent success of the USA's early warning and drug scene monitoring systems, we have no comparable apparatus in the UK. The voluntary urine testing of arrestees (Bennett, 1998) and the extension of this further into the criminal justice system will however produce a new and effective measure in due course.

Whilst the Misuse of Drugs Data Base could be upgraded and referral compliance improved, this system was not designed to be a free standing early warning indicator. Treatment data are best seen as validators of longer term trends.

In respect of enforcement, police arrest and conviction figures are useful but again because they are affected by so many organisational contingencies they cannot be relied on as a free standing indicator unless interpreted carefully and at the local level. Seizure data, despite being affected by unusually high or low seizures and strategic targeting, are however a relatively effective indictor of major changes or continuity in supply and thus as a reasonable predictor of emergent and manifesting drug scenes. Carefully interpreted seizure data combined with information on international drugs cultivation and trafficking does already make an effective indicator.

Basically, an effective early warning system would integrate several components and have reporters close to street level. The DAT/DRG system would make a useful vehicle for collating local data from outreach and front line workers and indeed users. Combined with information from Helplines, drugs researchers and doctors an impressive network could be established offering both local and national pictures. Unfortunately, in the immediate future there are likely to be other funding priorities and gaining full co-operation from all the potential participants would take several years.

In the absence of such a system one alternative – the rapid audit – can be utilised. This report provides a description of such an audit which was undertaken over a six month period, in order to establish whether 'rumours' of new heroin outbreaks amongst young people were fact or fiction.

3. Mapping the new heroin outbreaks

This section presents the results of a survey used to chart the extent of new heroin outbreaks amongst young people under nineteen reported by police forces, Drug Action Teams (DATs) and other key professionals in England and Wales. The section covers the following:

- setting up and conducting the survey – sampling and methodology
- mapping new heroin outbreaks – a national picture of the areas affected; and
- profiling the new young heroin user – defining demographic and social characteristics

It is important to recognise that the information contained in the tables and maps below is not based on hard data but on perceived 'spread patterns' of outbreaks reported by respondents and contacts in the areas covered by the survey although often supported by local data collection.

Setting up and conducting the survey

The questionnaire (reproduced at Appendix 1) consisted of a number of questions divided into five sections. Section one established the occupation of the informant and the geographical area in which they worked. Respondents were also asked about whether or not there was evidence of new heroin outbreaks in their area and how well placed they felt to assess the local drugs scene. In section two respondents were asked to list other key professionals in the area who may have relevant information about the local drugs scene. Section three was designed to establish the locations and scale of possible heroin outbreaks in addition to the nature of the supply and distribution of heroin. Sections four and five invited respondents to describe the extent of the heroin scene involving young people and to define the demographic and social characteristics of the new young heroin users.

During November 1997 a copy of the questionnaire was sent by post to the Chief Constables of the 43 police forces and to the chairpersons and co-ordinators of the 109 Drug Action Teams in England and Wales. The questionnaire was accompanied by a letter (see also Appendix 1) asking recipients to forward it to the relevant personnel or, as in the case of the DATs, to network key professionals in the local area. In total 208 questionnaires were returned of which 11 were completed via telephone interviews and 17 through face-to-face interviews (using the same questionnaire as the basis for an interview schedule). Five returns were discarded due to either too much missing data or invalid responses giving a final total of 203 valid returns. This relatively high response rate, giving good geographical coverage of the country, was achieved with follow-up telephone calls and letters to forces and DAT networks in February 1998[1].

Mapping outbreaks

Confidence and reliability

Establishing which areas are hosting new heroin outbreaks has been one of the main priorities of this survey. However, another and perhaps equally important task was to gauge how confident respondents felt about their own ability to assess local drug (and/or heroin) scenes. Was this survey/approach treated seriously by informants and could they assess their own ability to read the local drugs scene? With this in mind respondents were asked to indicate how well placed they were to report on any new heroin outbreaks (see question 5). For areas with more than one positive return, 'confidence scores' were added together and divided by the number of returns for that area. For example, in an area returning two questionnaires, one of which was rated with high confidence (3 points) and the other as low confidence (1 point), the scores would be aggregated and subsequently divided by two to give a final score of two points, and, therefore, a medium rated confidence score for that area[2]. Almost all respondents answered this question, giving us some basis on which to reach conclusions about validity.

Confidence rating was also partly instrumental in resolving *conflicts of opinion* where respondents from the same area returned questionnaires, independently of each other, indicating conflicting opinions about whether or not their areas were hosting new heroin outbreaks. In these instances conflicts were resolved by trying to check the veracity of claims made by the respondents involved. It was also thought necessary in some cases to assess the respondents' proximity to the local heroin/drug scene, their role within local professional networks and the details given by them before arriving at a final decision about how to represent such areas on the map. Cross referencing between police and DAT network returns and follow-up telephone calls was also helpful in this process.

The application of the confidence rating system was an important feature in formulating several of the maps below. Although it may have been possible to compile maps based simply on responses to Question 4, confidence rating allowed for the opportunity to add a further dimension to the picture. In the absence of any quantifiable statistics based on actual numbers of young people involved in outbreaks in a particular area the confidence rating system allows us to place more confidence in this type of analysis.

[1] *Initial recipients of the questionnaire were asked to forward it, if necessary, to other relevant professional personnel. In the absence of clear figures on the number of questionnaires forwarded in this way to potential respondents, we cannot assess reliably the actual response rate.*

[2] *Confidence rating system: low confidence = 1.00-1.66 points; medium confidence = 1.67-2.32 points; and high confidence = 2.33-3.00 points*

When reading maps 2, 3 and 4 it is important to note that areas **not** containing an encircled 'M' or 'L' symbol should be considered as high confidence rated area responses.

Heroin use in 1989
Map 1 represents notified addicts **per million** population by police force area in England & Wales in 1989. It gives a general impression of where the heroin outbreaks of the 1980s had the most impact. The largest concentrations were situated in the North West, Norfolk and Greater London. Other areas such as the South West, North Wales, Cumbria, South Yorkshire, Humberside, Cambridgeshire and parts of the south east also had considerably larger numbers of notified addicts than elsewhere. We include this map as a baseline of the geography of the 1980s outbreaks to compare and contrast with the current picture we create in this section.

Police
Map 2 shows areas containing new heroin outbreaks reported by police forces in England and Wales. A total of 52 valid questionnaires were returned by 37 of the 43 constabularies in England and Wales, representing an 86% area response rate.

Overall, 30 (81%) police forces reported new heroin outbreaks within their areas, four times that of those indicating no outbreaks (7 constabularies). Amongst the thirty force areas containing reported outbreaks 19 were rated with high confidence. These returns cover much of south to south-west England, the Midlands, Yorkshire and the North East. The returns from the remaining eleven outbreak areas were rated as medium confidence responses and are represented by an 'M' symbol. The majority of these are situated in the North West, central England and East Anglia.

Amongst those police force areas reporting no outbreaks within their boundaries, four were rated as high confidence returns with the remaining three returning medium rated confidence responses. Areas indicating no new heroin outbreaks were North Wales, Merseyside, Staffordshire, Gloucestershire, Dorset, City of London and Kent.

Of the 37 constabularies who returned questionnaires Northumbria and North Wales were the only forces where respondents had conflicting views regarding the scale of the current heroin scene within their respective areas. In the three questionnaires completed by Northumbria two respondents reported outbreaks, both with a high confidence rating, while the one indicating to the contrary was of

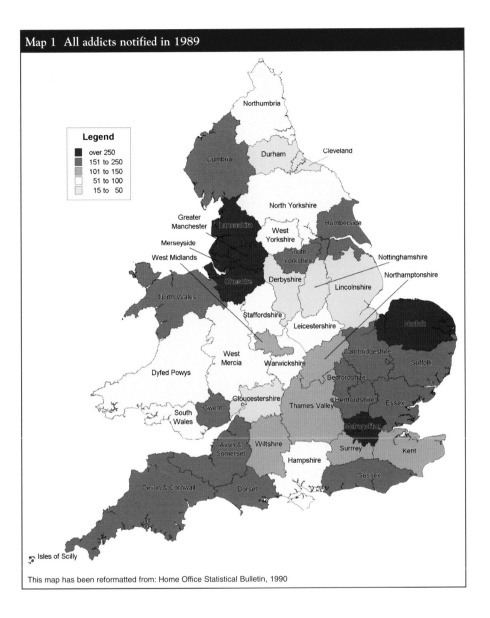

Map 1   All addicts notified in 1989

Legend
- over 250
- 151 to 250
- 101 to 150
- 51 to 100
- 15 to 50

This map has been reformatted from: Home Office Statistical Bulletin, 1990

medium level confidence. Therefore, in Map 2 Northumbria is represented as an area containing clusters of heroin outbreaks. In North Wales the conflict of opinion was conversely based on similar proportions, and therefore the area is represented in Map 2 as one containing no outbreaks.

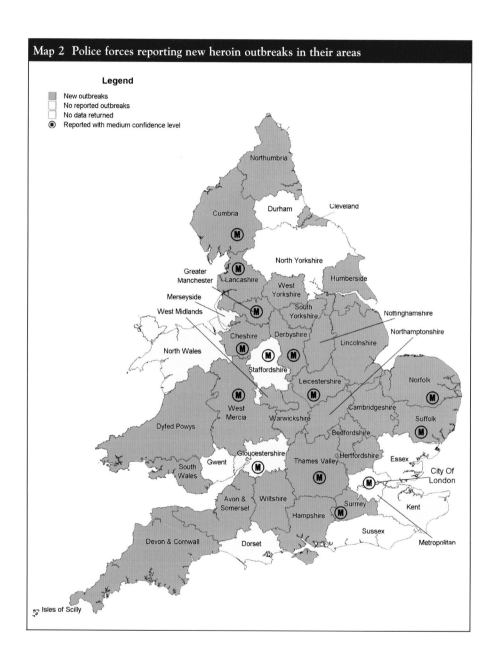

Map 2 Police forces reporting new heroin outbreaks in their areas

DAT network areas

Maps 3 and 4 show areas containing new heroin outbreaks reported by Drug Action Teams and local key professionals. A total of 151 valid questionnaires were returned by respondents from 79 of the 109 DAT areas of England and Wales representing a 73% area response rate. Almost half of the respondents were professionals employed by treatment and advice agencies, DAT co-ordinators represented about a fifth, and the remainder were youth workers, social workers, probation officers and health authority officers.

Overall, respondents from 63 (80%) areas reported heroin outbreaks within their areas, almost four times more than reported no outbreaks (16 areas). Amongst the areas containing new heroin outbreaks 36 were attributed a high confidence rating. Of the remaining 27 outbreak areas 24 were assigned a medium confidence rating (represented by an encircled 'M' symbol) and three with low confidence (represented by an encircled 'L' symbol). In the sixteen DAT areas where respondents reported no outbreaks only four were rated with high confidence whilst nine of the remaining were of medium confidence and three as low confidence.

Outbreaks reported by DAT network returns broadly mirror those shown in the previous map representing police force areas. Both the police and DAT networks indicate clusters of new and recent outbreaks in the South West England, the Midlands, East Anglia, West Yorkshire and parts of the North East. With the exception of North Wales, Gloucestershire, Staffordshire and Dorset the DAT networks also confirm police reports of heroin outbreaks in small cities and towns in some rural regions.

Map 3 Drug Action Teams reporting new heroin outbreaks in their areas

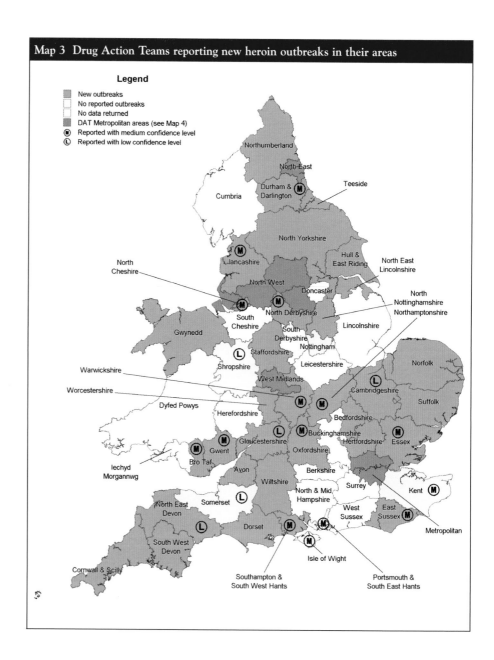

Legend

- New outbreaks
- No reported outbreaks
- No data returned
- DAT Metropolitan areas (see Map 4)
- Ⓜ Reported with medium confidence level
- Ⓛ Reported with low confidence level

Map 4 Drug Action Teams reporting new heroin outbreaks in their metropolitan areas

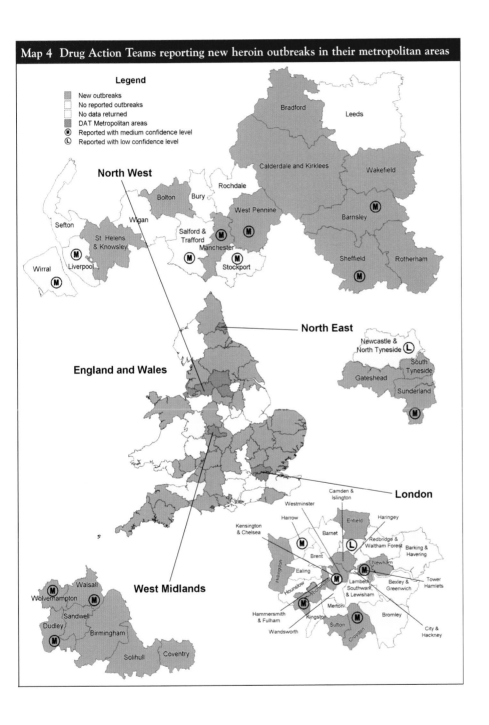

Legend

New outbreaks
No reported outbreaks
No data returned
DAT Metropolitan areas
Ⓜ Reported with medium confidence level
Ⓛ Reported with low confidence level

Profile of new young heroin users

The tables below are based on 165 returns given by police officers, DAT co-ordinators and other key professionals who reported new heroin outbreaks in their areas.

Age of young heroin users

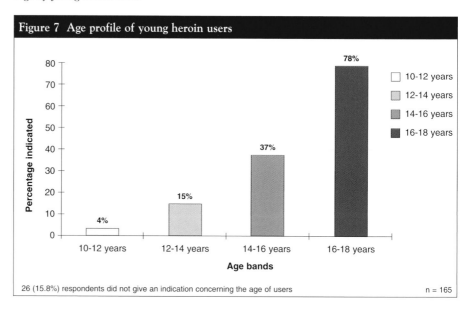

Figure 7 Age profile of young heroin users

26 (15.8%) respondents did not give an indication concerning the age of users   n = 165

Figure 7 shows the age profile of young heroin users. Respondents were asked to indicate one or more of the age bands listed which they felt best represented the age distribution of young heroin users in their areas. This is why the percentage figures shown above exceed 100%. Almost 80 % of respondents indicated that 16 and 18 year olds were involved. Over a third of respondents reported users aged between 14 and 16 while one in seven knew of users between 12 and 14 years old in their area. The youngest category was indicated by almost 4% of those reporting outbreaks in their areas.

The overall picture is that of 16 to 18 year olds being the modal age bracket but with significant numbers of mid adolescents also involved. Many areas noted their outbreaks also involved young people over the age of nineteen. This is an important issue but beyond the scope of our study.

Gender
44% of respondents said that the gender of heroin users under the age of nineteen was male. Although this was twenty times the amount indicating female (2%) a further 39% of respondents indicated both sexes as the main gender category[3]. This suggests that the majority of new heroin users are male but a significant minority of young women are also involved.

Ethnicity
Two thirds of respondents (66%) said users in their area were 'white'. The next largest category chosen was 'complex mix' (18%) followed by 2% 'Asian'. No respondents reported 'black' people as being the main user group[4]. As will become clear in Section 4, where towns experiencing full blown heroin outbreaks have an ethnic minority community living in its poorer neighbourhoods the young people from that community are affected.

Social characteristics of young heroin users
Respondents were asked to indicate which of the statements listed in Table 1 below best describes the social and economic circumstances of the young users in their area.

Table 1 Social characteristics of the young heroin use		
Statement	number indicated	percent
A: Primarily disadvantaged and deprived young people who may well be care leavers, excluded from school, homeless and sometimes involved in delinquency or the sex industry.	47	29
B: Primarily 'bonded' young people with intact families, school attending, not seriously delinquent. Probably have previous 'recreational' drug career.	12	7
C: A more complex or less clear picture	84	51
22 (13.3%) respondents did not give an indication concerning social characteristics of users		n = 165

Statement A was indicated by 29% of respondents – almost four times the 7% choosing Statement B. The most common indication was Statement C with just over half of respondents (51%) choosing this category. Many of those who chose Statement C commented that users in their area matched much of the profile described in Statement A with the exception of one or two of the criteria. For

[3] 22 (13.3%) respondents did not give an indication concerning the gender of users.

[4] 24 (14.5%) respondents did not give an indication concerning the ethnicity of users.

instance, several stated that users often came from stable but disadvantaged and economically deprived backgrounds, and were not involved in the sex industry. In retrospect this question could have been better worded. Our interpretation of the results, having read numerous comments, is that most heroin outbreaks primarily involve young people who **are** socially excluded or live in disadvantaged neighbourhoods. However, the picture is complicated by heroin use penetrating into other more affluent communities and attracting more middle class initiates from the serious end of the recreational drug use, sometimes found amongst night clubbers.

Methods of taking heroin

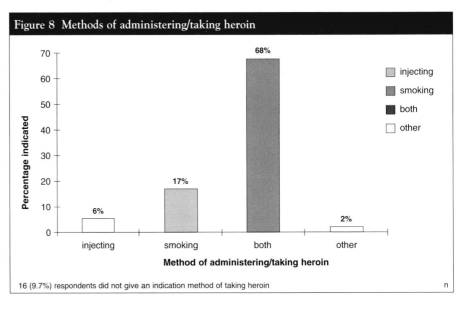

Figure 8 Methods of administering/taking heroin

16 (9.7%) respondents did not give an indication method of taking heroin

[5] *It should be noted that in addition to respondents being asked to indicate either 'injecting', 'smoking' or 'both' they were also asked to state, if appropriate, 'other' methods of administering heroin practised by young users in their areas. It is for this reason that that cumulative percentage values (including the value representing inappropriately missing responses) exceeds 100%.*

Figure 8[5] shows a distribution of the methods of administering heroin. Injecting was indicated by 6% of respondents as the main method of use representing less than a third of those reporting 'smoking' (17.0%). However, most respondents (68%) indicated that neither smoking nor injecting were used exclusively as the main method of taking heroin and that either or both methods were practised by significant numbers of users in their areas. Finally, three respondents (2%) reported the use of other methods of taking heroin, two of which stated 'snorting' while one stated 'oral'.

A speculative overview of the spread patterns

The distribution of areas containing heroin outbreaks shown in Map 5 represents a visual conclusion to the mapping process based on a summation of police force area and DAT network area returns. The compilation of this map made it possible to fill the gaps which appeared in the previous three maps above. Another reason for creating this map was to resolve any disagreement, within the same geographical area, between respondents representing the police and those from DAT networks who held contrary views about whether or not their areas contained new heroin outbreaks. Often decisions about how to represent these areas were made on the basis of comparing veracity of claims made by respondents and/or an evaluation of the respondents' proximity to the scene and their role in local professional networks. For example, in Greater Manchester the police reported heroin outbreaks (rated with medium confidence) but many of the returns from DAT networks did not concur with this view. It was therefore decided to represent Greater Manchester as containing no outbreaks in Map 5, with the exception of Bolton, upon which everyone agreed. The dissonance in areas such as North Wales, Somerset and Greater London was resolved in a similar fashion.

Map 5 Speculative overview of areas with reported heroin outbreaks

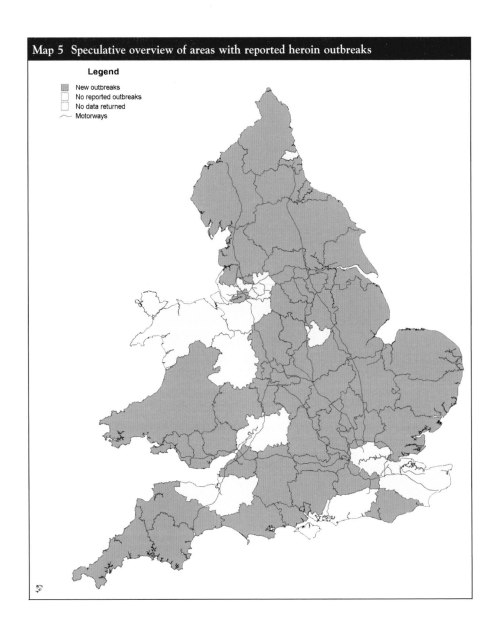

Legend

- New outbreaks
- No reported outbreaks
- No data returned
- Motorways

It is important to note that maps representing data from this survey are solely based on reported spread patterns of heroin outbreaks. In a few cases an area's shading on the map relies on the knowledge of one respondent reporting from a specific locality within its boundaries.

Finally, a note of caution is required in reading the situation in Merseyside, Greater Manchester and London. Whilst the survey returns lead us to conclude that these regions have no new substantive outbreaks we should remember that these areas host endemic long term heroin using populations. It is possible that this both camouflages new spread patterns and de-sensitizes professionals to recognising change.

Conclusions

There is little doubt that a second wave of new young heroin users is emerging in England and Wales. With 80% of area returns fairly confidently identifying new outbreaks within their communities and providing such a consistent picture and profile of new users it is, unfortunately, reasonable to suggest that we are facing a second heroin epidemic. This quick audit cannot quantify the depth of penetration of these outbreaks but the spread pattern is unequivocally consistent with an epidemic picture.

However when we compare Map 1 with 5 we can see an extraordinary change in the geography of heroin outbreaks. Those areas with no previous heroin history have become the sites of new outbreaks. Furthermore, some areas with a minor heroin history or footprint from the 1980s appear to have hosted major new outbreaks. Those regions, notably North West England and Greater London so deeply affected last time around report hardly any **new** outbreaks although clearly they continue to host an older endemic heroin/methadone using population. As we shall see in Section 5 this is no coincidence and the motorway network is superimposed on our speculative map for good reason.

The predominant profile of our new young heroin user also echoes with past experience. Heroin uptake is primarily found in the poorest estates and areas of our towns and small cities. The dominant profile of our users is thus associated with poverty, educational under-achievement and unemployment. Clearly we must view this profile as if it were a spectrum from that of the archetypal leaving care, homeless young person through to less alienated more conventional youth. However aside from those more 'bonded', 'stake holding' young people who try heroin via the recreational drugs scene or night club culture or because of personal predisposition, the linking of heroin and social exclusion can be a general rule of thumb once again.

The prevalence of injecting is also a major concern and as we shall see in the next section we are finding injecting amongst young initiates in several areas rather than the eventual transfer from smoking to injecting found in England during the last epidemic.

We can now begin to illustrate how outbreaks have been developing around the country on the basis of our fieldwork visits to a selection of towns and cities in England.

4. Local heroin outbreaks described

In this section we provide summary examples of the way new heroin outbreaks are colonising in cities and towns in England. These brief descriptions are based on fieldwork visits to a variety of areas in which key local actors, particularly drugs squad officers, DAT members and drugs agency staff were interviewed. We were also able to interview young heroin users (n = 13) through street level agencies in several areas and visit 'affected' neighbourhoods or estates.

In the last section we showed how the **majority** of urban areas in England are experiencing upturns in heroin use. Our site visits can thus only provide a means of illustrating and describing the way these outbreaks are developing around the country. Clearly we could have visited a completely different selection of areas as part of our fieldwork. Those cities and towns mentioned in this section are typical 'ordinary' places and to construe otherwise would be to grossly misinterpret the whole thrust of this report.

South West England

We showed in Section 3 that many parts of south west England have identified new heroin using scenes most notably coastal resort towns. However, the city of **Bristol** (population 385,000) is experiencing a full blown outbreak. It is one of several large towns/small cities with a heroin footprint from the 1980s which seems to have shaped and amplified its current outbreak.

The city went into the 1990s with several hundred adult opiate users and thereafter new, younger heroin initiates appear to have initially come from the city centre homeless and 'hostel' population which Bristol hosts. Local professionals mark out 1993-4 as the key period when this outbreak began. This chronology is confirmed by heroin seizure data, enquiries and referrals to its key drugs agency (Bristol Drugs Project), a major upturn in drug related offending and the development of numerous community action and self help groups in the city's poorest housing areas, desperately concerned about the growth of heroin use.

The heroin using population is found almost exclusively in the circle of housing estates which lie on the ring road around the city. The key outbreaks can be directly linked to a small number of major heroin dealers who purposefully set up in a couple of housing estates. One dealer who was convicted for his part in this had targeted young people from the in-care community. Despite the arrest of several key dealers, these outbreaks have spread right around the housing ring whereby local estimates of under 19s involved a range between 1,000 and 2,000.

Whilst young users tended to initiate as smokers there is a large and increasing injecting population emerging borne of a tradition of injecting amphetamines and a deterioration in the quality of street heroin in early 1997 which made smoking-burning ineffective and encouraged a switch to injecting.

The links with social deprivation are found not just in the geography of these heroin using clusters. The city's in-care adolescent population has been particularly affected and social workers have a clear profile of heroin and indeed poly drug use, embracing methadone and tranquillisers, amongst a significant minority of teenagers they are looking after. Many of these adolescents are becoming involved in petty crime. The links between heroin use and acquisitive crime which we find developing in the mid stages of a full blown outbreak are impacting on the local criminal justice system. Avon Probation Service believe that over 80% of the 18-25 year olds they have been working with because of burglary convictions have a drug problem dominated by heroin. Indeed the service has had to convert one of its hostels into a temporary rehabilitation centre given the problems of getting clients into treatment. One manager felt heroin, and to some extent cocaine, "is the biggest thing to hit the drugs scene in the past four years".

Finally Bristol's struggle to create a sufficient treatment response illustrates the difficulties which many other areas will face. The area has no detoxification facilities for under 18s and has hardly any specialist mental health-drugs services beyond Bristol Drugs Project. Consequently treatment responses have been both hidden and displaced in that local GPs have responded in an **ad hoc** manner, many prescribing methadone and tranquillisers to young users who have **not** had a specialist assessment. We interviewed young users who were receiving prescribed methadone, tranquillisers and still using street heroin and who were already poly-drug users with no immediate prospect of being given access to a detoxification service. The tendency for heroin users to become poly-drug users is thus being inadvertently facilitated by a lack of specialist services and a reliance on GPs who understandably, given their lack of specialist knowledge, respond by immediate prescribing, but often with no clear, broader intervention plan.

North East England

Whilst the city of Newcastle has not yet seen substantive increases in heroin use, numerous towns in the region are hosting heroin outbreaks but are at quite different stages of diffusion. Thus some towns like Blyth have seen their outbreak peak after several years of high incidence but others like Gateshead and Hartlepool are currently experiencing the epidemic rise. We will discuss the significance of the heroin distribution 'chain' in Section 5 but in the north east we find

Newcastle, and particularly Middlesborough, play a key role as wholesale depots linking the supply bases (e.g. Leeds and Liverpool) with the local outbreak towns.

Blyth (population 35,000) has had more than its share of publicity in respect of its heroin, but more appropriately poly-drug using problem, embracing methadone and tranquilliser use, often through injection. There is a particularly complicated situation in this town which we do not pretend to fully understand. What is clear is that unlike many other towns from Berwick in the far north east right down across the region, which are currently in the early stages of the outbreak, Blyth has weathered several difficult years with overdose deaths, crises of confidence about treatment responses, a heroin-crime link and a now small endemic population of young dependent combination drug users, most of whom are injectors. The town has learnt by trial and error that great care must be taken with prescribed drugs and its methadone service is now highly regulated through carefully chosen pharmacies.

Gateshead is typical of numerous middle sized towns just coming to terms with the fact it has a growing heroin problem in sections of its youth population. The town (92,000) has seen a rapid diffusion of heroin use which began in 1994-5. The arrival of heroin has aggravated the already difficult adolescent drugs scene in the town, whereby the heavy use of alcohol and the regional commitment to misusing tranquillisers, 'wobbly eggs', has been further complicated by 'brown'. Police intelligence suggests a small number of very well organised mobile phone and home based dealers are setting up in the town's estates selling £10 and occasional £5 bags of heroin. Most young users are smoking their heroin and professionals working in the area feel that dependency levels are, as yet, low. Smoking 'brown' is currently perceived by many young users as an extension of their drugs careers based on alcohol, cannabis, solvents/gases, amphetamines and minor tranquillisers.

In the understandable absence of specialist detoxification and treatment services Gateshead is attempting to link together GPs with what specialist drugs services it has. As yet, however, the town has, like so many others, no clear picture of the scale of the user population and thus a foundation upon which to plan its response. This town illustrates the complexities of these new outbreaks in that heroin is superimposed on an already serious 'depressant' recreational drugs scene, the outcome of which is as yet unclear.

Teeside saw an increase in heroin use in the early 1990s amongst its twenty something population. However around 1993-5 there were clear signs that sections of the youth population in numerous towns (e.g. Hartlepool, Saltburn, Stockton) were starting to try heroin. Middlesborough not only hosts outbreaks but is the dealing/distribution base for the surrounding towns. Its supplies come mainly from Leeds and Liverpool and the police also believe that small sections of the area's Asian community are involved in supply.

The region is currently seeing all the indicators of more widespread heroin use pointing upwards in terms of drugs seizures, police arrests, referrals to drugs agencies and a doubling of the NHS methadone prescribing bill in only a few years. Recorded crime rates are not rising however and the local police view is that most drug related crime is currently 'hidden' in shoplifting and user-dealer income generation. These heroin outbreaks have given an urgency to the search for corporate decision making across the region, although we sensed an agreed strategy was some time away.

Hull and East Riding

Moving down the coast we find a similar situation with towns across East Riding (e.g. Goole, Bridlington) experiencing new outbreaks. The region's capital Hull (240,000) is unfortunately experiencing a full scale local outbreak and again this seems linked to a footprint from the 1980s. Hull first saw heroin in about 1985 in the west of the city. During the late 1980s this area was redeveloped, fragmenting the heroin community and perhaps facilitating some spread of heroin use. Heroin use grew only slowly until 1994 when the city began to see a new outbreak. This outbreak has an unfortunate mix of the classic epidemic patterns discussed in Section 1, exacerbated by the immediate adoption of an injecting culture by initiates (found in the city via the older heroin users and amphetamine injectors) and aggressive supplying and dealing from outside the area, notably from Merseyside, utilising local small time dealers and users-dealers to increase turnover.

The picture is particularly bleak given Hull has a large susceptible population living in areas of relative poverty, poor housing and an under performing educational system now linked with an injecting culture and a very young user population. The package of 'social' problems associated with such a development outbreak have already emerged in Hull. A drug using care leaving population, pregnancies amongst young female users, a major problem with injecting equipment and signs of a growth in acquisitive drug related crime are all further driven by purposeful aggressive dealing.

There are considerable efforts being made to develop a corporate response. However, the difficulties in defining the scale of the problem, said to be measured in thousands, bringing on board medical services and resolving the knotty dilemmas about methadone prescribing and providing clean injecting equipment are understandably slowing progress. This region undoubtedly faces a long and problematic period ahead.

The Yorkshire Region

Whilst only small pockets of new heroin use were reported in North Yorkshire the survey found that South Yorkshire and particularly almost all of West Yorkshire are being affected by outbreaks. Whilst Bradford's problem demanded a fieldwork visit the smaller towns we visited merely illustrate the spread problem. We deliberately visited areas only beginning to see the impact of a local outbreak, rather than concentrating only on those towns (e.g. Barnsley) reporting serious difficulties. Once again we see the significance of the supply and distribution bases of the cities (e.g. Bradford and Leeds) in facilitating the development of heroin availability in small towns throughout the region, often initially marketed at rock bottom prices.

Dewsbury exemplifies the plethora of towns in England and Wales with no heroin history, which escaped the 1980s outbreaks and now suddenly find themselves with a young adult and youth population of users. We should not expect a town of only 50,000 even with a fully developed outbreak to host more than a couple of hundred users and, given the town's key drugs agency (Unit 51) reports the outbreak beginning in 1992-3 with increased referrals through to the present involving over a hundred young people, there must be some hope that heroin use will have spread as far as it is going to in this town. The initial profile of the town's users matches the social exclusion picture found in the survey, however professionals working in the town report the increasing appearance of more 'bonded', affluent, young problem users. As one well placed drugs worker notes, this may indicate a wider penetration whereby "everyone I know tells me that heroin is becoming a cool drug to use. This second wave appear to be buying their heroin from the first wave, the apostles of heroin". Consistent with this fully developed outbreak, services are finding, given the town's ethnic mix, a significant proportion of young female and Asian users.

The spread of heroin use in the Yorkshire region will continue for some time and numerous towns are only beginning to hear and see signs of its arrival. **Huddersfield** (125,000) is probably seeing the early signs of heroin use develop in its youth and young adult population. An arrest referral scheme and an effective street level drugs agency both indicate increases in young heroin users. We found that it was those professionals closest to the street (e.g. the uniformed police officer, the outreach worker) who had anecdotal evidence of the growth of heroin dealing and use.

Turning now to **Bradford** (population 295,000) we have another city experiencing a full blown outbreak and yet again an area with a footprint from the 1980s. Bradford saw the arrival of heroin in the 1980s (Pearson et al, 1986) and went into the 1990s with several hundred adult opiate users living around the city. In 1992-3 the city saw a classic epidemic outbreak involving large numbers of disaffected young people primarily from the poorest areas of the city. The scene is extremely complex however with not only young unemployed/out of school white males but an increasing proportion of young women and penetration into the Asian youth population (see Pearson and Patel, 1998).

Bradford has very well established drugs services, notably two methadone prescribing schemes and the more broad based services of the Bridge Project. Whilst the local DAT has made young heroin users its primary concern, the city's long heroin history and relatively strong service sector (aside from detoxification facilities) means that those dealing with the heroin problem are more sanguine than elsewhere. Aside from a fierce debate about the extensive use of methadone prescribing to new young users, there is a sense of a corporate approach to the city's drug problem and an overt awareness it can at best be managed rather than eradicated.

West Midlands

By and large the West Midlands was surprisingly unaffected by the 1980s outbreaks. However the survey suggests that each of its metropolitan boroughs is now seeing outbreaks of varying scale. As a key English city **Birmingham** (1,024,000) obviously hosts some heroin using networks created in the mid 1980s but this relatively small endemic population remained stable right through until about 1996 when, local professionals agree, a major influx of heroin began perhaps on the back of the arrival of crack cocaine a little earlier. Large 'kilo' suppliers quickly and efficiently distributed heroin to the city and region wide dealers. Street level dealing is currently primarily conducted through the use of mobile phones and again anecdotal reports of slick '2 bags for £15' marketing are legion. Treatment centres throughout the region report increased referrals. As one drugs worker put it "phone call after phone call from concerned mothers saying their children and all their friends are using heroin". Whilst the dominant picture of social exclusion remains, there was a strong sense of the situation being more complex with heroin use being reported in the club scene and with some take up in middle class recreational drugs arenas.

With all the metropolitan areas of West Midlands reporting new outbreaks, the region ideally deserved extended fieldwork visits but this was beyond our brief audit. Certainly we found that Solihull had an emerging problem with heroin now available in the town. Dudley and Walsall reported an upsurge of young heroin users and a significant fall in price but not purity. In other parts of the region, notably Sandwell, the picture was less clear although an increase in heroin use was noted. In Coventry the extension of heroin use alongside a strong amphetamine using culture is occurring. In Wolverhampton there are a number of indicators to suggest that heroin use has been increasing amongst young people. A new young persons' service is currently being set up and has received 15 referrals in six weeks. The youth justice and social services teams have reported that many of their clients have heroin/drug problems. Another sign which indicates that there is a problematic drug scene is the number of young female sex workers involved with heroin.

South East England

Our audit was at its least effective in respect of describing the situation in Greater London and the south east. Our assumption is that the lower response/return rates from the region indicate that heroin outbreaks are less common or certainly less recognised. Even based on returns from this region, we showed earlier that a smaller proportion of areas reported new heroin outbreaks. One area we visited was **Luton** (population 166,000) in Bedfordshire. The town has large ethnic communities of Indian, Pakistani and Bangladeshi residents accounting for about 13% of its population. It has several deprived wards and is seen by commentators as something of a transit town given its geography and position on the M1. All the indicators including seizures and treatment data bases suggest heroin use has been increasing significantly in Luton. Professionals we interviewed confirmed this but felt the rise was difficult to quantify. They were clear that the ethnic minority population was affected by heroin but felt this remained hidden. With relatively few services to monitor problem drug use and a smoking rather than injecting 'culture', there were few available measures of the scale of heroin use.

A fairly elaborate dealing system dominated by mobile phone ordering and dealing was described. Purity levels are high in the town and Luton airport was perceived as an additional supply mechanism for the area. Luton was also defined as the distribution site to supply other towns in Bedfordshire (e.g. Milton Keynes and Leighton Buzzard).

Conclusions

These brief descriptions of local heroin outbreaks can only give an outline impression of what is occurring in most areas of England and similarly in some areas in Wales. We could have quite feasibly undertaken our fieldwork in other counties or regions and produced a similar picture, at least in respect of small and middle sized towns. Currently rural areas, notably parts of West Wales, well away from major transportation/travel routes, those areas with no pockets or sectors of socio-economic deprivation and the old heroin cities of Liverpool, London and Manchester, are the best 'protected'. However the key conclusion is surely that any community can be susceptible to some penetration if not through its poverty zone then through any serious recreational drug and club scene.

The other key conclusion is that it is hard quickly to identify new outbreaks at the local level and almost impossible to quantify them without specialist research. Thus slow problem definition delays response time and blunts the potency of a corporate response even with the DAT structure in place. By the time the heroin users 'present' in the criminal justice system or at the drugs agency, the outbreak is well established. GPs are one key professional group with some ability to give an early warning. However we found the familiar pattern in most areas we visited in that they are neither organised nor inclined to spontaneously report patient referrals. Moreover, their temptation to immediately prescribe methadone and often tranquillisers in the absence of well established specialist referral procedures has its own consequences (see Section 6). The understandable general absence of young people's drugs services around the country will undoubtedly become a major public policy issue in the very near future.

Finally, the heroin supplying and distribution networks alluded to in these local cameos are in fact found nation-wide and such is their significance in stimulating and feeding the heroin outbreaks that we must now attempt to define them more accurately.

5. Distributing and dealing heroin for new markets

The distinctive patterns and geography of these new heroin outbreaks described in the previous sections cannot be fully explored or explained by this small investigation. However because this study has spanned the whole of England and Wales and because there is such a consensus and integrity in the data we do offer an outline explanation as to how these outbreaks have developed in relation to supply and distribution. The outline model can then be further tested and re-worked as our collective knowledge about contemporary heroin distribution and marketing increases.

Basically there are currently three components in place which have allowed these outbreaks to develop and be sustained. They are illustrated in Figure 9. We begin by considering why youth populations, at the end of the decade, may be particularly susceptible to trying heroin. We then look briefly at how heroin has become far more widely imported into the UK whereby a supply system delivering cheap, pure heroin has bedded in. The drug supply and the potential customer base must then be linked by a distribution system. The simultaneous and largely unorchestrated construction of the contacts, channels, routes and bridges which make up this distribution network have been developing rapidly since the mid 1990s. This means we can now identify a sophisticated, and adaptable and thus highly effective heroin distribution and dealing industry.

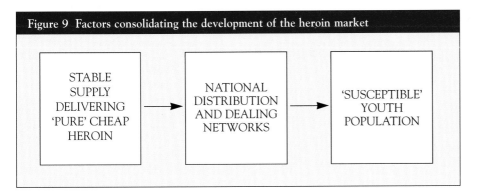

Figure 9 Factors consolidating the development of the heroin market

STABLE SUPPLY DELIVERING 'PURE' CHEAP HEROIN → NATIONAL DISTRIBUTION AND DEALING NETWORKS → 'SUSCEPTIBLE' YOUTH POPULATION

Susceptible youth populations

Cyclical moments
The heroin outbreaks of the 1980s suggested that only a small minority of any youth and young adult population are susceptible to heroin trying or use. Even at their height, in affected urban areas, the 1980s outbreaks rarely involved more than 10% of the then 16-25 'at risk' population. And even

then the most affected areas and populations had a distinctive profile related to social and economic deprivation.

The impact of heroin use in creating folk devils of the users was very real. The majority of the wider community saw 'smackheads' and 'junkies' as beyond the pale and the stereotype was only further amplified by the HIV/AIDS panic of the late 1980s, when needle sharing was identified as a key transmission route of the HIV virus. Perhaps due to this imagery one of the repeated findings of drugs surveys of youth populations in the UK through the early 1990s was the **rejection** of heroin as an acceptable drug to even try. Despite having increasingly diverse 'recreational' drugs appetites most 1990s youth have rejected 'hard', 'addictive' drugs such as crack cocaine and heroin (Parker et al, 1998). Indeed, as far as we know, no UK representative youth surveys during the 1990s have recorded more than two or three percent lifetime trying of heroin until these current outbreaks began to impact (Aldridge et al, forthcoming).

Unfortunately the protective value of perceiving heroin for what it is, a highly addictive drug, appears to have 'worn off' with each age cohort. Thus by and large those who grew up in the late 1980s and early 1990s have moved into adulthood with strong anti-heroin images and attitudes. However for those who were small children during the 1980s and are today's teenagers there is no recollection that 'heroin screws you up' and little fear of HIV/AIDS. With few public health campaigns even mentioning heroin and with the emphasis on cannabis and ecstasy in public and political discourse it is unsurprising that the 'fear' and understanding of the damage regular heroin use can trigger may have reduced.

This is not to suggest that most young people do not still define heroin as a dangerous drug. They do, but some now do so in a rather abstract way often comparing it with ecstasy (Measham et al, 1998). This formalised rather than animated rejection of heroin suggests increased susceptibility amongst young cohorts is occurring particularly when we add other risk factors.

Our basic argument, following on from the first heroin wave described in Section 1, is that we have now reached another historical moment when the factors which have been 'protecting' young people from heroin are fairly weak. (Must we bemusedly accept the cyclical logic of heroin outbreaks? (Hunt and Chambers, 1976)). The world has changed greatly in the past 15 years, however, and post modern, 1990s youth are far more *drugwise* and drug experienced than their predecessors and we cannot be sure how this will reshape epidemiological outcomes over the next few years. It was certainly one of our initial hypotheses that if heroin became packaged or defined in a certain way then there is some risk of its use extending into the wider recreational drugs scene (dominated by the less addictive; cannabis, amphetamines, LSD and ecstasy).

Susceptibility
Within the general youth population who are the most likely to try heroin? Firstly, we must accept that serious drug users tend to score distinctively and away from the norm on various attitudinal and personality measurements, for instance sensation seeking. Another way of casting this is to talk about early risk takers who smoke, drink and experiment with drugs in late childhood and early adolescence and see no reason to desist. There are far more of these early risk takers than there will be new heroin users. However, if we place these early risk takers on the social exclusion backcloth, then we can see susceptibility become operationalised (ACMD, 1998). There is little doubt that if we add poor school performance and attendance, light parental supervision and growing up at the wrong end of town, then we are offering a basic identikit of the most likely heroin user.

This is the largest susceptible group. If we place them at the centre of the susceptibility spectrum then at the highest risk end we must add the care leavers, young homeless and institutionalised offenders. At the other end we have the 'serious' early recreational drug users who otherwise have conforming characteristics. They are likely to be in school, in training or in work and reside within well functioning families. The survey did suggest some penetration here but the data were rather anecdotal. The use of heroin as a chill out drug in the dance drug scene was the most often reported example of uptake but with no sense of this becoming a widespread practice.

The single biggest worry is that the opportunity to try heroin is being presented in **early** adolescence when young people have insufficient drugs and life experience to make informed choices. We have seen a drop in the age of onset of all illicit drug trying in recent years, alarmingly so in some regions (McKeganey, 1998). If we pair this with the fact that a significant minority of the under 19s profiled by our survey were described by local returners as under 16s, then we must adjust the most 'at risk' age group this time around to **14-25** years. Moreover, if we do find widespread susceptibility through the recreational drugs scene, then our one in ten susceptibility in the at risk age range will be too conservative.

In summary, we have reached an historical moment when we once again have a susceptible minority within our youth population. We can outline their defining criteria but cannot yet quantify the likely scale of penetration. The least worst scenario is that heroin trying does not become accommodated within the far larger 'recreational' drugs scene but remains predominantly associated with degrees of social exclusion. This whole issue needs careful monitoring and profiling.

Supplying heroin to the UK*

This section has been written using material provided by HM Customs and Excise National Intelligence about global drug production and trafficking.

Another way the world has changed since the 1980s is that there has been enormous increase in global trade. As legitimate trading has demanded and been enhanced by improved road and rail links and especially with the containerisation of freight linking sea, road and rail routes, so too drug trafficking is assisted. As air travel grows and people routinely fly all over the world so too couriers can move more easily and with less risk of detection. As we see the beginnings of free movement right across Europe including the old Soviet Union and Eastern European States so the transportation of drugs is facilitated. As we take down EU frontiers and build new bridges and tunnels and transport links between member states so we bolster illegal as well as legitimate trade. In short we have in place so many ways of transporting drugs between supply and consumption countries that one can now quickly and easily stimulate the other even though they are many hundreds of miles apart.

Upon this post-modern backcloth we must face the fact that the world wide production of almost all illicit drugs is increasing and that crop cultivation of coca and poppy plants is increasing annually with more sophisticated farming techniques allowing up to 5 yields a year in countries like Thailand. There is also evidence, for instance because of the decline in the USA's crack cocaine market, that cultivation countries can quickly switch crops. Thus various South American countries are currently transferring from coca to poppy.

The UK market is supplied primarily by the countries of south west Asia. Turkish processing and the role of Turkish criminal networks in organising transportation appears crucial. The main trade route is Balkan or, more accurately, the myriad of routes and modes of heroin movement are across Eastern into Western Europe. The legitimate trading infrastructure outlined above creates the medium for smuggling from the air traveller courier, to the car, the yacht and the awesome possè of TIR lorries. The potency of this trafficking industry appears to be increasing with international intelligence suggesting previously separate trafficking groups are now networking with each other. Moreover the ability of the traffickers to respond to surveillance or threat by re-routing and using new modes of delivery is acknowledged by intelligence sources.

In short there is little doubt that since about 1993-4 the supplies of heroin coming into the UK have increased significantly. This is indicated in several ways. Heroin seizures both by Customs and Excise with record levels since 1995 and police seizures over 100% in 1996 on 1995 figures are indicative. Purity levels remain high with little cutting (Coomber, 1997) whilst the retail price has fallen significantly, a clear sign of strong availability.

Distribution and dealing

The distribution networks

The distinctions we have made between the old heroin sites (eg London, Manchester and Liverpool) the towns with heroin for the first time since 1994-5 and the small cities/large towns which went into the 1990s with a heroin 'footprint' continue to be important.

The repeated 'public intelligence' from the survey returns is that the heroin supplies, the wholesale depots, are found in the cities which had epidemics during the 1980s and thus have established heroin supplying and dealing systems. The kilos rest in these cities guarded by well organised criminals, many working independently and some almost alone and it may be no coincidence that city suppliers have not stimulated a demand for heroin in their own back yard. Manchester supported by Bradford and Leeds for instance are the primary supply bases for the north and north east of England. Liverpool not only 'trades' with the north of England but Wales and indeed the coastal resorts of south west England. Wherever we find towns with outbreaks we find the nearest big cities have a role and the old site cities are, in turn, usually involved. In short the big suppliers who work with the 'kilos' are usually geographically removed from both new markets and young customers. For these suppliers, whilst they may have difficulties over turf, trading and taxing in their own cities there is very little risk or indeed contact with the dealing bases currently consolidating in the affected towns. The trade goes both ways with some pretty big quantities being moved by the city suppliers to the newer market or the 'ounces' men travelling to the supply cities. The image of numerous different sized consignments of heroin being moved backwards and forwards down the motorway networks by small time distributors unbeknown to each other is not fanciful. There is a clear relationship between transport routes and the new outbreaks (see Map 5, Section 3).

Dealing in the towns
There is a remarkable similarity in the survey returns describing the dealing systems which act as the conduit between the suppliers and the susceptible population. Fieldwork visits involving interviews with police officers and drugs workers and indeed heroin users confirm this picture.

Whilst some open markets were reported these, because of their visibility, were few and were quickly closed down by local police action. The two main semi-closed market systems (Edmunds et al, 1996) operating are the home based dealer and the mobile dealer. Neither of these dealing systems are new nor indeed unique to heroin. Both normally require potential buyers to be 'vetted' before being given access to an address or phone number.

The home based dealers provide an *in situ* service to heroin users and new initiates. Some will be long-standing dealers who have diversified from cannabis and amphetamine selling to boost profits, others will have purposefully set up to sell heroin and create a regular customer base. In time, during full blown outbreaks, users will in turn become dealers to fund their habits.

With the widespread use of pagers and mobile phones the mobile dealer offers an alternative by providing customers with 'home delivery' or 'deals on wheels'. Basically customers once accepted can ring the dealer who will either deliver the dose by car or by using a third party either to the punter's home or an agreed drop off point (car park, pub, etc). The third party may be another user or often a young person acting as a runner or, in reality, biker. The gross gains shown in Figure 10 are handsome because it is at this lowest level that the work, 'the graft', is hardest and the risks and incidental costs highest. This said we should note that our city suppliers and main town dealers will conduct several 'wholesale' transactions a week thereby grossing far more than the illustration in Figure 10.

Figure 10 Schematic example of heroin distribution at regional level	
	Gross Gain
City-regional suppliers with access to kilos – sells five ounces to a main town dealer for £3,000. One transaction will produce	£500
↓	
Main town dealer delivers and sells in one ounces to five estate/local level dealers for £800 an ounce. Five transactions will produce	£1,000
↓	
Local small-time dealers cut and wrap 280 x £10 bags from their ounce to retail directly to the users. Each 'grosses' before costs, £2,000 so in total these five will produce	£10,000

Repackaging heroin at the point of sale
Several small cities/large towns which went into the 1990s with established heroin
using and dealing communities and have been particularly badly affected since
1993-4 because of this footprint. However, there is a strong sense in this outbreak
of heroin finding **new** sites in new ways. Whilst the dealership systems may not be
new the manner in which heroin is named, packaged and priced is. There is
indisputable evidence that heroin has been re-defined and specifically marketed to
appeal to a new younger potential 'towny' market. Firstly, there are numerous
reports of heroin being renamed as 'brown' or 'browns'. Secondly, although there
are several areas where heroin initiation is via injecting, most young people are
introduced to brown as a smokable powder. Indeed building a 'spliff' to smoke
heroin rather than 'chasing the dragon' is, by mimicking the primary way cannabis
is ingested, another sales feature. Thirdly, the almost universal price of a wrap of
brown is £10. This is typically the same price as an ecstasy tablet, a wrap of
amphetamine and a decent cannabis deal. The message of course is that heroin is
apparently no more expensive and little different than other 'recreational' illicit
drugs. With numerous reports of new markets being created with the sale of £3 and
£5 wraps it is clear that the market ploys of high street retailers have not been lost
on the 'cornershop' drug traders.

By and large purity levels of heroin being imported (40-60%) whilst not always
maintained, do not appear to fall below 20% during the regional distribution and

cutting. Clearly however because this is an uncontrolled market local variations occur. A few areas reported that ruthless dealing at the 'estate' level meant purity got below 10% in the final wrap. Cutting usually involves paracetamol or glucose. The amount of heroin found in the £10 wrap varied from 1/10 down to 1/16 of a gram.

Discussion

Our provisional conclusion is that the heroin outbreaks spreading across Great Britain are primarily a product of purposeful supplying and marketing. The precursor to all of this has been the strong, sustained availability of pure, inexpensive heroin primarily from south west Asia. The price for an effective, legitimate, global economy and a relaxation of migration and citizenship regulation appears to be the development of equally potent illegal market making and supplying mechanisms.

We have also concluded that the second half of the 1990s has seen the coming of age of new cohorts of youth with little knowledge or informed awareness of the distinctiveness and addictiveness of heroin. Most new heroin users will be *drugwise* but based on their own and their peers' extensive use of cannabis and the dance drugs. This is of little assistance in helping them assess heroin, indeed given the way heroin has been marketed at the street level to tune into the 'recreational' drugs scene it is possible that the extensive non opiate drugs experience of contemporary youth may well have undermined resistance.

The blatant marketing of heroin as 'browns' as smokable, as rather like cannabis and in £5 and £10 wraps reported so extensively in the survey is but one aspect of the elaborate and aggressive distribution system for heroin which is currently consolidating itself. Whilst traditional distribution and dealing networks have expanded or diversified to include heroin selling it is the development of an 'infinite' number of new dealerships which is spreading heroin use and making the bridge to susceptible youth. The impact of post-modernity with pagers and mobile phones, mountain bikes and cars with shaded windows is strong. It combines with the strategic marketing whereby the kilos are found in the cities and old heroin areas but the 'ounces' men, the small time dealers and user dealers are **in situ** in the towns where heroin use is to spread and where the turf, taxing and the gun waving of the city suppliers' world is, initially, largely absent. This is an adapted version of macro-diffusion whereby the motorway networks in particular allow supplies and suppliers to travel many hundreds of miles and in a wholly strategic way. The profits to be made for the hard working, well organised distributor are considerable. This carrot explains the resilience, flexibility and replicability of the illegal market makers and traders and makes successful intervention particularly challenging.

The relatively recent development of this more sophisticated heroin distribution system and its increased ability to 'service' small towns and previously relatively heroin free regions was clearly a source of frustration to many of the specialist drugs police officers we met with. Two issues stood out.

Firstly, most acknowledged that the removal of a town or estate level heroin dealer, whilst it satisfied local demand from residents or councillors, often had little lasting positive effect in that replacement dealers quickly sprang up and often in new locations beyond immediate intelligence. Stemming the flow of heroin into a particular neighbourhood, unless at the very early stages of a heroin outbreak, is extremely difficult to achieve. There may be scope for a more integrated and comprehensive approach at 'town' level whereby creating a heroin drought is part of a much wider strategy involving housing officials (see ACMD, 1998), local residents' groups, schools and drugs services. This might involve plotting exactly what heroin users would do in a particular area in drought conditions. Would they travel elsewhere for supply and where? Would and could they transfer to street methadone, tranquillisers or cannabis? Might they seek help from a local service and could a peripatetic service be taken to them?

The second issue involved policing the distribution system from the kilos down to the street deals. As we have reported there is a clear awareness of the distribution routes and transportation devices being utilised, most notably the strong reliance on the motorways network. This is full blown 'cross border' crime and poses genuine difficulties for enforcement requiring as it does continuous and extensive inter and cross force co-ordination and co-operation and expensive surveillance (Porter, 1996). Perhaps inevitably more rural areas with apparently smaller drugs problems are also neglected in this respect (Davidson et al, 1997).

What is clear is that cheap, relative pure heroin is reaching new youth populations in new areas on a continuous basis. Given what we know about the life cycle of heroin outbreaks and the dependent heroin users' strategies for feeding expensive habits, it does follow that greater priority should be given to disrupting the national distribution networks. We should not underestimate the difficulties involved however since this would require NCIS, the National Crime Squad and all local police forces to work together in a sustained way and even then with no guarantee that the processes of replacement and displacement would not undermine their efforts.

Finally, although very little hard evidence emerged from this study about the development of drugs-crime careers in these new young heroin users 'rumours' were rife. It is likely in the early stages of local outbreaks that this link will be forming only slowly and will anyway initially be 'lost' in unreported shoplifting. However there is little doubt that the components are there for a drug related increase in acquisitive crime to occur in the next few years. Much will depend on how quickly and effectively we respond to these new outbreaks. One key issue will be how we develop services for the new waves of young heroin users.

6. Developing new services for young heroin users

In this section we attempt to link the implications of these new heroin outbreaks with the wider debates about young people's drug services and drugs education. Our perspective is that, in the end, and despite the damage that young problem drug users may cause others, we must attempt to provide caring, high quality services for them. There are several reasons for this. Firstly, if every citizen is to be a stake holder and if social exclusion is to be minimised, in keeping with both government and EU goals, then we here have a population demanding our attention. Secondly, we know that certain treatment regimes are effective in terms of individual recovery or stability (NTORS, 1996). Thirdly, we know that major intervention programmes although they appear expensive to the purchasers are in fact cost effective for a town, city or society, when compared with the costs of collateral damage of treating poor health, heroin related social and personal problems and drug related crime. Doing nothing or simply relying on punitive responses via the criminal justice system is in the end the most expensive option (Hough, 1996). Indeed the potency of the law and order debate means that we already have strong research led initiatives being developed, supported by new legislation, in respect of drug using offenders. Although there will be pressures on adult services as a consequence of these outbreaks, we limit ourselves here to under 19s. Basically what we do not have is a network of young person's drug services, and for this reason and because this will undoubtedly become the priority at the local level over the next few years, we concentrate on service responses.

There is already a realisation that young person's drug services must become a priority development. We find this in the Health Advisory Service's **Children and Young People: substance misuse services** (1996) the Social Services Inspectorate's **Substance Misuse and Young People** (1997) and SCODA's **Policy Guidelines for Working with Young Drug Users** (1998). Set alongside the government's new drugs strategy and commitment to developing young person's drug services all these reports provide a reasonable consensus on what framework is required and how to develop young person specific services. The discussion here is meant to complement this wider debate.

All the above mentioned reports are packed with sensible suggestions and guidelines. They also provide a schematic framework to facilitate smooth development at an inter-agency level. However it is only when discussing the drugs problems of adolescents leaving care or being looked after by the local authority that we actually hear about the drugs misused and the multiple problems of these young people. More generally there is an absence of detail about what we are dealing with. Yet it is the detail, in the realities of young people's drugs problems and lifestyles, that the dilemmas arise. Consequently we feel it important to spell out the sorts of issues which any 'successful' front line young people's drugs service must face in response to the early and middle stages of a substantive local heroin outbreak.

Facing up to unattractive alternatives

Pro-active responses
We sensed a frustration amongst many front line police officers and more particularly drugs service managers in the heroin outbreak areas we visited. They felt they could not get 'the system', the inter-agency partnership, to galvanise its responses. Yet the lessons from the 1980s outbreaks are clear. The realities are best faced voluntarily sooner rather than, under pressure, later. Heroin careers wait for no one, they have a long life and if unchecked or unchallenged the harm moves beyond the user, his or her family and on into the wider community. Your town ends up with high rates of shoplifting, acquisitive crime, drug dealing, dangerous injecting debris and angry residents. Caseload pressure on social services, probation, the courts, primary and secondary health services grows. Consequently so does corporate stress amplified by the local media demanding more from city hall.

We currently have towns and small cities at different stages of outbreak development. Some as we have seen are attempting to manage full blown outbreaks, others can expect the worst while those areas where heroin has just, or will shortly arrive, have more time to co-ordinate and galvanise their managerial strategy. Unfortunately and with a few exceptions most heroin outbreak areas lack the appropriate service infrastructure. However, if this were not enough those areas which bite the bullet and set about building up a long term response strategy will find themselves confronted with a host of legal, moral, ethical and political dilemmas. We are convinced that, despite the difficulties, those areas which take a pro-active, corporate, long term approach to challenging their heroin outbreaks whilst caring for young (and indeed young adult) heroin users will in five years time, be grateful they did.

'Treatment' dilemmas
The framework documents referred to above all address the legal dilemmas of providing confidential services for under 16 year olds. However where we have substantial clusters of young heroin users these dilemmas quickly multiply. Should pharmacists refuse giving sterile injecting equipment to young people because they look under 16? How should a drugs agency respond to a desperate, aggressive parent who literally drags a crying daughter in, demanding her heroin use ceases now? What should a young user from an ethnic minority do if he wants help but cannot trust the local doctor not to tell his parents?

Such dilemmas will become routine, ironically, as service development improves and more young users present from the hidden sector. However the biggest dilemma of all will involve making a decision about the dominant treatment regime for heroin dependency-methadone prescribing. This issue cannot be fudged.

There is already a growing debate about methadone prescribing in respect of current adult services. Basically we are now realising that despite the very considerable benefits of methadone (a carrot to keep people in services, crime reduction, client stabilisation, reduction of illicit drug use) we have not managed to wean the previous heroin generations off their 'meth'. Indeed if we had we might not have current service provision fully occupied and blocked with long term twenty and thirty something client-patients. The libertarians and critics of methadone will rightly remind us of this and question whether we wish to submit adolescents and young adults to such a regime, to a chemical cosh, which might in the end act to prolong a dependent drugs career. In fact we will find many young heroin users reject methadone out of hand but many others won't and will happily become scripted. Methadone will probably continue to play an important role in managing these new outbreaks hopefully most often with those young users who have not managed to get off heroin in the first few years, in maternity cases and for those committing serious regular crime and who are picked up in the criminal justice system.

However this is quite different from endorsing prescribing as a first step. Yet this is already exactly what is happening up and down the country with GPs prescribing methadone and benzodiazepines, and routinely before specialist assessment. This say some is potentially the road to poly problem drug use not abstention. This issue must be resolved and clear advice and guidelines given to local areas which will otherwise become entangled in intense debates and disagreements.

Developing services for young heroin users

Starting points for service responses to heroin outbreaks
There are already some pockets of good practice with young heroin users but by and large we must assume that the development of new services will be a growth area in the next few years. The trick will be to combine what we know about treatment effectiveness with what we know about the life cycle of heroin outbreaks and associated drug careers with what we are learning, for the first time, about the presenting agendas of new young heroin users. We know least about this latter profile because we have never seen such a young population using heroin and because we are unclear how the wider youth drugs scene, so

potent during the 1990s, will mediate their heroin use. The generation gulf between youth and their elders over drugs also clouds the picture.

It is beyond our current brief to pull all this together but on the basis of our understanding of the last heroin outbreaks and the profile of younger users gleaned from this study we do feel the need to warn of the magnitude, complexities and difficulties which lie ahead and which are eerily missing from the service reviews quoted earlier. In our view the biggest danger for service development is to underestimate the level of professional expertise which will be required to set up effective new services without serious mishap (MORI, 1997).

Basically what is likely to happen, but which in our opinion should not, is that these new services will be built under the umbrellas and in the style and the traditions of the old. Our view is that in many areas we should start again because to put it bluntly the medical-methadone orientation of current specialist services and the 'laid back' style of so many current street agencies are both inappropriate, particularly in combination. We believe that this time around heroin careers should be **challenged**, particularly in such a young population rather than consolidated by the substitution of heroin with methadone unless as a detoxification tool. If the challenge is unsuccessful then methadone prescribing remains a secondary option – an unattractive but acceptable option not least because an alternative was offered and tried. On the other hand we are dealing with a new largely socially excluded population of heroin users, from modern times, who bring with them some raw life experiences and plenty of attitude. It would be contradictory and counter productive to create a new service which alienates them further and consolidates their negative views about the local state by challenging them too hard, too soon. One solution may be in a person centred **tough love** approach which draws in young heroin and combination drug users at different stages of their drugs careers yet most of whom will not be contemplating giving up heroin. There is usually a one-five year gap between heroin initiation and seeking 'treatment'. However if we broaden our perspective and accept that these young heroin users, certainly in the early stages of their drugs career, will have far more diffuse personal and social problems and will have problems with use (eg infected injection sites) rather than being chaotic dependent users, then we have the foundations of a longer term strategy.

We know that the pre-requisite to effective treatment is sustaining contact with the 'client' for several months (Hough, 1996). In the absence of the methadone carrot the way to produce this contract of contact is by creating a user friendly young person's service with demand led service entry. This is the love. This is also the intake system which starts pulling in the users from the outbreak areas.

Creating an intake service

This service has several complementary goals. As well as trying to meet the needs of heroin users at different stages of their careers it also provides a monitoring and intelligence system to guide local strategy and inform future service development. A successful service will attract a sufficient number of young users who can in turn be co-opted to help (and be rewarded) in assessing the scale of 'hidden use', the propensity for injecting, the problems users are facing, attitudes to methadone treatment and so on. Thorough assessments made gently over several visits will also allow local strategists to predict which specialist services may need developing, whether they be a non-chemical detox programme or a social and employment skills programme to move stable users onto. Even an enormous 'did not re-attend' profile is educational.

Our new drop-in service is discretely housed in a non residential area but with good public transport links and close to the town centre. It has a comfy waiting area with smoking and a non-judgemental receptionist. Copies of **Mix Mag** not **Women's Own** sit alongside educational leaflets. The notice board is up to speed and up to date. The service has long opening hours focusing on afternoon and evening peak demand. It has a 24 hour telephone helpline. There is no waiting list (Bell et al, 1994) and a weekend emergency service. Missing appointments is not a hanging offence and no correspondence is sent to the client's home without prior permission. There is a separate entrance to the needle exchange (if required). Young clients are encouraged to drop in to this facility when they wish. There are rules and sanctions but the style is very young person centred and reasonably forgiving.

Set up in this way in the early to mid stages of a local heroin outbreak and if promoted properly (eg flyers in pubs, clubs, cafÈs, local adverts, referrals from inter-professional networks) this service is likely to be fairly generic. Some young people will come in wanting information about heroin, about the 'facts' of poly-drug use and injecting. Some will be having trouble at home with parents, quarrels with 'clean' friends. Should they begin drug dealing how can they make £20 a day? Should they let their friend inject them for the first time, what can they do about withdrawals when they can't get any heroin, or they're going away from town? Is it true what they hear about methadone? And so on.

Assuring quality and responsiveness

We should not underestimate the degree of professionalism required to run such a service successfully. Based on the picture from the survey and our fieldwork assessments it is likely that many service users will be very challenging. Many will be excluded from school or have left school early with no qualifications. They may well thoroughly distrust people in authority and expect to be put down by adults. They will quote their experiences at home, at school, on the street, in the Bridewell and at the Youth Court as evidence that no-one gives a damn.

This is not a caricature and it is why we have said that those areas which commit to a long term strategy of service development will initially find the politics of implementation particularly painful. The fundamental message is that in setting up such a service purchasers should be willing and able to aim for the most able staff and commit to a budget in which recruitment, staff development, monitoring and evaluation are of the highest order. This alas is not the current norm given the plethora of short term funding sources (e.g. Lottery Board, European Social Fund, Single Regeneration Budget) and lack of uniform quality assurance mechanisms.

The sort of young persons' service described here will have to walk the political and legal tightrope, the more so the more successful is its intake service and retention rate. Moreover it will need to develop in parallel to the life cycle of the heroin outbreak creating more demanding and challenging interventions as the 'first wave' either contemplate moderation or abstention or become more entrenched in problematic 'chaotic' drugs careers. It thus, in time, becomes a referral agent attempting to encourage or push longer term clients into more specific treatment or counselling options or on good weeks into recovery programmes and employment schemes. It also remains as the intake system until incidence, the waves of new users, falls back. This might take three to five years.

Public health messages
This sudden return of heroin especially into youth populations was not widely predicted. Given the epidemic diffusion period is far from over it seems sensible to attempt to dissuade heroin trying through prevention messages alongside some secondary prevention or harm reduction messages for new to heroin users.

Heroin has hardly been mentioned in the 1990s public health/drugs education campaigns targeted at young people through schools, in magazines, leaflets and via radio and TV campaigns. The focus has been on amphetamines and ecstasy and attempting to influence age cohorts of 1990s youth, half of whom have tried an illicit drug and a quarter of whom are more regular primarily 'recreational' users of cannabis and the dance drugs (POST, 1996; ISDD, 1997; Parker et al, 1998). Consequently, however apparently drugwise today's youth are, early and mid adolescents know very little about heroin and its dependency potential. Whilst the credibility of such drugs education messages may have been undermined by the tendency to lump all drugs together – as wrong and dangerous – there should nevertheless, be an attempt to give heroin a bad name.

Because it is unlikely that heroin use will spread beyond a minority of any youthful cohort then we can set our targets as 11-25 year olds but with a focus on the groups at greatest risk and found on the susceptibility spectrum outlined in the last section. In early and mid adolescence we know that those being cared for, those not in school and early 'risk takers', who begin alcohol and tobacco use around 10-12 with early cannabis and solvent/gases trying, should be our target groups. In later adolescence we know that social exclusion on the one hand and extensive 'recreational' drug use may correlate with heroin trying.

Clearly there will need to be different messages and different mediums for these distinctive groups and since they will in most cases be fairly drug experienced the messages will have to distinguish between heroin and the other drugs. Implicitly if not explicitly these campaigns will have to acknowledge a hierarchy of dangerousness in which heroin is many Richter points up the scale from cannabis. This truth cannot be fudged not least because the vast majority of cannabis users will never try heroin but the vast majority of heroin triers and users also smoke cannabis. Here again the recent politicisation of drugs policy will make this necessary innovation controversial. Here again we would argue that there is a public health imperative, as with HIV/AIDs, which should override the objections.

Summary

There will undoubtedly be a rapid growth in young person's drugs services over the next few years. In terms of dealing with young heroin users there are good reasons to resist building on the styles and regimes of current adult services. Instead new, innovative, service provision should be attempted using carefully selected and supported staff who recognise the massive significance that providing a welcoming, accommodating and client retaining service holds. The added value of a street level intake service comes in being able to gear assessment to both the individual and defining the scale and nature of the local outbreak. Beyond the intake system a number of specialist service routes should be set up. There should be a robust quality assurance system for these new services whoever funds them.

A public health/drugs education campaign aimed at giving heroin a bad name by outlining its addictiveness and the lifestyle it tends to pull users into should also be attempted, taking account of the characteristics of those most at risk on the susceptibility spectrum.

References

ACMD (1998) *Drug Misuse and the Environment* Advisory on the Misuse of Drugs, London: Home Office.

Aldridge, J. and Parker, H. (forthcoming) *Adolescent drug trying and drug use in two Northern Regions.* Report to the Drugs Prevention Initiative, Home Office.

Balding, J. (1997) *Young People in 1996* Exeter: Exeter University.

Bell, J., Caplehorn, J. and McNeil, D. (1994) 'The effect of intake procedures on performance in methadone maintenance' in *Addiction*, 89 pp. 463-471.

Bennett, T. (1998) *Drug Testing Arrestees.* Home Office Research Findings 70, London.

Bottomley, A.K. and Pease, K. (1986) *Crime and Punishment: Interpreting the Data.* Milton Keynes: Open University Press.

Brain, K., Parker, H. and Bottomley, T. (1997) *Evolving Crack Cocaine Careers: new users, quitters and long term combination drug users in NW England.* London: Home Office.

Carlen, P. (1996) *Jigsaw – A Political Criminology of Youth Homelessness.* Buckingham: Open University Press.

Coffield, F., Borril, C. and Marshall, S. (1986) *Growing Up At The Margins.* Milton Keynes: Open University Press.

Collison, M. (1996) 'In search of the High Life: Drugs, Crime, Masculinity and Consumption' in *British Journal of Criminology* 36, 3, pp 428-444.

Coomber, R. (1997) 'How often does the adulteration/dilution of heroin actually occur' *The International Journal of Drug Policy* V8, 4, pp. 178-186.

Davidson, N., Sturgeon-Adams, L. and Burrows, C. (1997) *Tackling Rural Drugs Problems* Crime Detection and Prevention Series Paper 81, Police Research Group, London: Home Office.

De Alceron, R. (1969) 'The spread of heroin in a community' in *Bulletin on Narcotics*, July-Sept., pp. 17-22.

Department of Health (1998) *Statistical Bulletin: Drug misuse statistics for six months ending September 1996*, March 1998, Issue 05/98. London.

Dorn, N., Ribbens, J. and Smith, N. (1987) *Coping with a nightmare: family feelings about long term drug use*. London: ISDD.

Edmunds, M., Hough, M. and Urquia, N. (1996) *Tackling Local Drug Markets*. London: Home Office, Crime Detection and Prevention Services, Police Research Group.

Edmunds, M., May, T., Heardon, I and Hough, M (1998), *Arrest referral: emerging lessons from the research*. DPI paper 23. London: Home Office

Fazey, C. (1987) *The Evaluation of the Liverpool Drug Dependency Clinic 1985-7*. Liverpool: Mersey Regional Health.

Gay, M. et al (1985) *The Interim Report: Avon Drug Abuse Monitoring Project*. Bristol: Hartcliffe Health Centre.

Gossop, M., Griffiths, P., Powis, B. and Strang, J. (1993) 'Severity of heroin dependence and HIV risk' in *Aids Care* 5, 2, pp 159-168.

Graham, J. and Bowling, B. (1995) *Young People and Crime*. Home Office Research Study 145, London: Home Office.

Griffiths, P., Gossop, M., Powis, B. and Strang, J. (1994) 'Transitions in patterns of heroin administration' in *Addiction* 89, pp 301-309.

HEA (1998) *Needs to Know: the needs of local professionals and Drug Reference Groups in their work with young people, parents and drugs*. Report for the Health Education Authority, London (unpublished).

Hammersely, R., Forsyth, A., Morrison, V. and Davies, J. (1989) 'The relationship between crime and opioid use' in *British Journal of Addiction* 82, pp. 899-906.

Hartnoll, R. et al (1985) *Drug Problems Assessing Local Needs*. Drug Indicators Project, London.

Haw, S. (1985) *Drug Problems in Greater Glasgow*. Glasgow: SCODA.

Hickman, M., Sutcliffe, H., Sondhi, A. and Stimson, G.V. 'Validation of a regional drug misuse database: implications for policy and surveillance of problem drug use in the UK' in *British Medical Journal* 315.

Home Office (1997) *Statistical Bulletin: Statistics of drug addicts notified to the Home Office, United Kingdom, 1996*, 14 October 1997, Issue 22/97, London. (Prepared by J. Corkery).

Home Office (1998) *Statistical Bulletin: Statistics of drug seizures and offenders dealt with, United Kingdom, 1996*, 9 April, 1998, Issue 10/98, London.(Prepared by J. Corkery).

Hough, M. (1996) *Problem Drug Use and Criminal Justice*. London: Drugs Prevention Initiative.

Hunt, S. and Chambers, C. (1976) *The Heroin Epidemics: a study of heroin use in the United States*. New York: Spectrum

ISDD (1994) *Paying for Heroin*. London: Institute for the Study of Drug Dependence.

ISDD (1997) *Drug Misuse in Britain 1996*. London: Institute for the Study of Drug Dependence.

Jarvis, G. and Parker, H. (1989) 'Young Heroin Users and Crime' in *British Journal of Criminology* 29, pp 175-185.

Kearney, P. and Ibbetson, M. (1991) 'Opiate dependent women and their babies: a study of the multi-disciplinary work in a hospital and a local authority' in *British Journal of Social Work*. 21, pp 105-126.

Kleber, H. (1988) 'Epidemic Cocaine Abuse: America's Present, Britain's Future' in *British Journal of Addiction* 85, pp 1351-1371.

Klenka, H. 91986) 'Babies born in a district general hospital to mothers taking heroin' in *British Medical Journal*. 293, pp 745-6.

McKeganey, N. (1997) *Pre-teen Drug Users in Scotland*. Glasgow: University of Glasgow. Unpublished.

Miller, P. and Plant, M. (1996) 'Drinking, smoking and illicit drug use among 15 and 16 year olds in the United Kingdom' in *British Medical Journal* 313, pp 394-397.

MORI (1997) *The Effectiveness of Services for Young Drug Users* Report to the Department of Health, London.

NTORS (1996) *The National Treatment Outcome Research Study*. London: Department of Health.

Parker, H. and Bottomley, T. (1996) *Crack Cocaine and Drugs Crime Careers*. London: Home Office Publications Unit.

Parker, H. and Kirby, P. (1996) *Methadone Maintenance and Crime Reduction on Merseyside*. London: Police Research Group, Crime Prevention Series.

Parker, H., Aldridge, J. and Measham, F. (1998) *Illegal Leisure: the normalisation of adolescent recreational drug use*. London: Routledge.

Parker, H., Bakx, K. and Newcombe, R. (1988) *Living with Heroin: the impact of a drugs 'epidemic' on an English Community*. Milton Keynes: Open University Press.

Pearson, G., Gilman, M. and McIver, S. (1986) *Young People and Heroin: an examination of heroin use in the North of England*. London: Health Education Council.

Pearson, G. and Patel, K. (1998) 'Drugs, Deprivation and Ethnicity: Outreach among Asian drug users in a northern English city' in *Journal of Drug Issues*, 28, 1, pp. 199-224.

Porter, M. (1996) *Tackling Cross Border Crime*, Crime Detection and Prevention Series, Paper 79, Police Research Group, London: Home Office.

Power, R. et al (1992) 'The role of significant life events in discriminating help seeking among illicit drug users' in *The International Journal of the Addictions*. 17, 9, pp 1019-1034.

Ramsay, M. and Spiller, J. (1997) *Drug misuse declared in 1996: latest results from the British Crime Survey* Home Office Research Study 12, London: Home Office.

Roberts, C., Moore, L., Blakey, V., Playle, R. and Tutor-Smith, C. (1995) 'Drug Use Among 15-16 year olds in Wales, 1990-94' in *Drugs: education , prevention and policy*. 2, 3, pp 305-317.

Stares, P. (1996) *Global Habit: the drug problem in a borderless world*. Washington: Brooklyn Institute.

Stimson, G. and Oppenheimer, E. (1982) *Heroin Addiction: Treatment and Control in Britain*. London: Tavistock.

Stutman, R. (1989) 'Crack Stories from the States' in *Druglink*. 5, 4, pp 6-7.

Appendix 1

HP/DM

Re: **Heroin Outbreaks Amongst Young People**

To: Chief Constables England and Wales.
           Chairs/Co-ordinators of Drug Action Teams England and Wales.

We have been commissioned to undertake an audit of any information and intelligence about recent/new outbreaks of heroin use amongst young people under 19. There is some evidence to suggest that there are 'hot spots' developing in several areas of the country. A rapid audit and thus an 'early warning' system is required, to respond to what would be a serious deterioration in the drugs problem at a local level.

This investigation has the full support of the Association of Chief Police Officers and the Central Drugs Co-ordination Unit. It is funded by the Police Research Group at the Home Office.

The enclosed questionnaire takes only a few minutes to complete. Unfortunately directing copies to the appropriate key individuals in your organisation or professional network is more demanding. Please can you think of anyone else, aside from the person to whom you would normally delegate the completion of this questionnaire, who may be particularly well placed to know about young people who may be using heroin. Could you please send an additional copy of the questionnaire to them.

We will be making fieldwork visits early next year around the country. We are concentrating on areas where heroin outbreaks have been identified to try and make a more sophisticated assessment of each local situation and thereby build up a national picture.

As this is only a short project we do need to have these survey returns by Christmas. We would therefore be very grateful if you would authorise the completion of these questionnaires as soon as possible and ensure their return as best you can.

Thank you for your co-operation.

Yours sincerely,

PROFESSOR HOWARD PARKER
Roy Egginton
Catherine Bury
Research Fellows

NEW HEROIN USE AMONGST UNDER 19s
SIGNS AND INDICATORS QUESTIONNAIRE

SECTION 1

Please complete this short (10 minute) questionnaire as fully as you can. A 'no evidence', no signs, return is as important as one indicating young people's heroin use, so please complete all relevant sections whatever your assessment. Any requests for anonymity or confidentiality will be honoured.

1   Please state the exact overall area you are referring to (e.g. Lancaster only, all Lancashire)

2   Which DAT covers your Area?

3   Have you heard and accepted any 'plausible' claims or been persuaded by any evidence etc. that heroin trying and use (whatever other drugs they also maybe using) by young people has developed or grown in your Area over the past 2 years?

No ☐
Yes ☐

4   Please can you state your position:

Occupation

Role or Rank

Contact Phone Number

5   How well placed do you feel you are able to assess the drugs scene and any new developments? (please tick one)

(a)	Very confident because I feel well placed to read the local drugs scene	☐
(b)	Reasonably confident because I have some knowledge of the local drug scene	☐
(c)	It is possible my view is inaccurate as I am not ideally placed	☐

SECTION 2:

OTHER PEOPLE IN YOUR AREA WHO MIGHT HAVE RELEVANT INFORMATION

6   **Please list any other people in your area who you think may be well placed to make an assessment of the nature and scale of heroin use amongst young people.**

(a)   **Professionals**

Name	Position/Agency	Telephone Number

1.

2.

3.

(b)   **Lay People (e.g. key residents, local activists)**

Name	Role or Setting	Telephone Number

1.

2.

3.

(c)   **Other Information/Informants**

If you have access to young drug users, dealers or other informants,

please can you indicate whether, after negotiations and arrangements are acceptable to you or someone else, they might be contacted?
Please describe these in your own words.

. . . .

. . . .

. . . .

. . . .

If you answered **NO** to Question 3. Thank you for completing this questionnaire. Please return it with any other comments you wish to make in the envelope provided.

If you answered **YES** to Question 3 please continue to complete the questionnaire.

SECTION 3:

THE LOCATIONS AND SCALE OF POSSIBLE HEROIN 'OUTBREAKS'

7   What are the locations or sites of possible heroin use within the area you are representing? (e.g. town X but particularly neighbourhood Y)

	Location	Focal Point of Use
1.		
2.		
3.		
4.		

Please comment

. . . .

. . . .

8   How many young heroin triers and users, under 19 years, do you think might be involved across the overall area
(i.e. all locations within) you are representing?

Please comment on your estimation

. . . .

. . . .

. . . .

<u>Heroin Supply and Distribution</u>

9   Please describe the heroin supply scene involving young people as best you can. Please include any information about *purity, price, type of deal*, (e.g. £10 wraps), *nature of distribution*, (e.g. phone orders, street market, home based dealers).

. . . .

. . . .

. . . .

. . . .

. . . .

. . . .

SECTION 4:

NATURE OF THE HEROIN SCENES
INVOLVING YOUNG PEOPLE

10   Please describe how these heroin using scenes have evolved. Include anything you know about the origins, development and scale of the scene.

. . . .

. . . .

. . . .

. . . .

. . . .

11   What methods are being used to take heroin? (please tick as appropriate)

Injecting ☐   Smoking ☐   Both ☐   Other ☐

☐ ☐ ☐ ☐

SECTION 5:

CHARACTERISTICS OF YOUNG HEROIN USERS

12   **What are the age, gender and race characteristics of the new users?**

Age		Gender		Ethnicity	
10-12 years	☐	Mainly Male	☐	Mainly White	☐
12-14 years	☐	Mainly Female	☐	Mainly Black	☐
14-16 years	☐	Both Sexes	☐	Mainly Asian	☐
16-18 years	☐			Complex Mix	☐

(tick where appropriate)   (tick one only)   (tick one only)

Please comment

. . . .

. . . .

13   **What statement best defines the characteristics of these new young heroin users you have identified?** (please tick one)

☐   Primarily disadvantaged and deprived young people who may well be care leavers, excluded from school, homeless and sometimes involved in delinquency or the sex industry.

☐   Primarily 'bounded' young people with intact families, school attending, not seriously delinquent. Probably have previous 'recreational' drug career.

☐   A more complex or less clear picture.

Please expand:

. . . .

. . . .

. . . .

Thank you for completing this questionnaire. Please add anything else you think appropriate below. Please send any material you think suitable. All information will be treated sensitively and with great care. Use S.A.E. enclosed.

Professor Howard Parker, Ms. Catherine Bury and Mr. Roy Egginton, SPARC, 4th Floor, Williamson Building, University of Manchester, Manchester, M13 9PL. Tel: 0161-275-4777/4912. Fax: 0161-275-4922. E-mail: sparc@man.ac.uk

Please add any Comments, Suggestions, Ideas about this issue you care to make

....

....

....

....

....

....

....

....

....

....

....

....

....

....

Appendix 2: Research, monitoring and evaluation needs

- There is a strong case for undertaking a similar audit for Scotland. Given recent concerns about the arrival of heroin in Northern Ireland a modified audit might also be appropriate.

- Further monitoring of the development and spread potential of these outbreaks is required. In particular uptake of heroin amongst 'bonded' recreational drug users needs assessing.

- This report only details the spread pattern. We need to quantify the numbers of new heroin users involved, probably using capture – recapture techniques, in several different outbreak areas.

- The impact of these outbreaks on Asian communities needs exploring.

- There is a need to describe the range of time phased 'harms' from the outbreaks by studying those towns/small cities with full outbreaks so that other areas at an earlier stage can prepare their responses to issues like drug related crime, pregnancy, maternity/child care, dealing with an injecting culture and a move into heavy end poly-drug use which is a likely eventual outcome of these heroin careers.

- Current good practice knowledge needs bringing together and disseminating to local areas who have already declared their 'need to know' more about drugs scenes, intervention effectiveness etc. (HEA, 1998). Armed with a thorough knowledge about the life cycle of a heroin outbreak and what works (and does not) in terms of treatment and enforcement, local partnerships could be far more effective.

- The effectiveness of 'taking out' heroin dealers at the local level remains unclear. An evaluation or review of how best to police supply and distribution in areas at different stages of their heroin outbreaks would be timely. The issue of 'cross border' policing in respect of challenging the heroin distribution system also needs further attention.

RECENT POLICE RESEARCH GROUP CRIME DETECTION AND PREVENTION SERIES PAPERS:

73. **Forensic Science and Crime Investigation.** Nick Tilley and Andy Ford. 1996.

74. **Policing Problem Housing Estates.** Sheridan Morris. 1996.

75. **Problem-Orientated Policing: Brit Pop.** Adrian Leigh, Tim Read and Nick Tilley. 1996.

76. **Shop Theft: Improving the Police Response.** Helen McCulloch. 1996.

77. **Solving Residential Burglary.** Timothy Coupe and Max Griffiths. 1996.

78. **Armed Robbery: Two Police Responses.** Roger Matthews. 1996.

79. **Tackling Cross Border Crime.** Mike Porter. 1996.

80. **Tackling Local Drug Markets.** Mark Edmunds, Michael Hough and Norman Urquia. 1996.

81. **Tackling Rural Drug Problems: A Participatory Approach**. Norman Davidson, Louise Sturgeon-Adams and Coral Burrows. 1997.

82. **Biting Back II: Reducing Repeat Victimisation in Huddersfield.** Sylvia Chenery, John Holt and Ken Pease. 1997.

83. **Keeping Track? Observations on Sex Offender Registers in the U.S.** Bill Hebenton and Terry Thomas. 1997.

84. **Policing Racially Motivated Incidents.** Warwick Maynard and Tim Read. 1997.

85. **Getting the Grease to the Squeak: Research Lessons for Crime Prevention.** Michael Hough and Nick Tilley. 1998.

86. **Clubs, Drugs and Doormen.** Sheridan Morris. 1998.

87. **Tackling Street Robbery: A Comparative Evaluation of Operation Eagle Eye.** Janet E. Stockdale and Peter J.Gresham. 1998.

88. **The Nature and Extent of Light Commercial Vehicle Theft.** Rick Brown and Julie Saliba. 1998.

89. **Police Anti-Drugs Strategies Tackling Drugs Together Three Years On.** Tim Newburn and Joe Elliott. 1998.

90. **Repeat Victimisation: Taking Stock.** Ken Pease. 1998.

91. **Auditing Crime and Disorder: Guidance for local partnerships.** Michael Hough and Nick Tilley. 1998.